Here is a volume that will help both healthy and hurting families to find victory in the spiritual battle in which all Christians are engaged. While some aspects of the book may seem foreign to sheltered believers, *Reclaiming Surrendered Ground* provides practical, biblical counsel on how to live on the victory side both individually and as a family.

J. Ronald Blue, Ph.D.
President, CAM International

As I travel to the nations of the world to preach the gospel, I sense that the intensity of the battle for the hearts of people is growing rapidly. The heart of the battle in the West seems to be the family. As nations and as individuals we have given up much ground to the enemy. Jim Logan's book is very timely, theologically sound, and greatly needed. He points us to the ground in our lives and families that have been surrendered to Satan. He then directs us to biblical and practical solutions to reclaiming that ground. I heartily commend this book to Christians everywhere.

Sammy Tippit
Author, International evangelist

Jim Logan speaks and writes from a background of extensive study, reading, teaching, and ministry experience. He makes a very significant contribution to the current discussion on the on-going, spiritual conflict between our Lord and His people on the one side and Satan and his followers on the other. This book should be read and studied widely in the church, and its principles and guidelines implemented.

Dr. Timothy M. Warner
Author, Teacher

PROTECTING
YOUR FAMILY FROM
SPIRITUAL ATTACKS

RECLAIMING SURRENDERED GROUND

JIM LOGAN

MOODY PRESS
CHICAGO

*to my beloved wife, Marguerite, who has
stood by my side for more than 40 years
and to our four children and their spouses:
Cheryl and Tom,
Teri,
Wendy and Tim,
Richard and Diana,*

*and our six grandchildren:
Michelle, Sarah, Elizabeth,
Jeremiah, Rachelle, and Malachi*

CONTENTS

INDEX OF "HIGHER GROUND" STEPS

FOREWORD

As Christians we are engaged in intense warfare with our implacable enemy the devil, the one whom the apostle Paul calls "the prince of the power of the air" (Ephesians 2:2).

Because Satan and all his forces are spirits, our battle is a spiritual one and our weapons must be spiritual weapons. That's exactly what Paul says in 2 Corinthians 10:3–4: "For though we walk in the flesh, we do not war after the flesh: (For the weapons of our warfare are not carnal, but mighty through God to the pulling down of strong holds)."

And to make sure we understand the intensity of the struggle we are engaged in, Peter reminds us that "Your adversary the devil, as a roaring lion, walketh about, seeking whom he may devour" (1 Peter 5:8). If the devil did not shrink from tempting Jesus to disobey His heavenly Father in the wilderness, and if the devil plotted through evil men to destroy Jesus on the cross, we can be sure he will not hesitate to attack us.

However, we do not have to fear our enemy and his schemes. Praise God, through His death and triumphant resurrection the Lord Jesus Christ has secured the victory for us over Satan and the forces of evil (2 Corinthians 2:14; Colossians 2:15). Our privilege, our assignment, is to stand in the victory Jesus gives, keeping our eyes fixed on Him (Hebrew 12:2).

But the devil is a shrewd enemy. He has been tempting God's people for centuries, putting traps and snares in our path to get our eyes off Jesus and onto ourselves and our circumstances. When that happens, we are sure to stumble and fall.

The devil tempts us in many ways, and his methods differ with each of us because he knows the point of our weakness. Whether it's immorality, dishonesty, bitterness, or pride, he knows what it takes to snare us. And the nature of sin is such that if we do not deal with sin and fortify these areas of weakness, we will continue to experience spiritual defeat.

This is why I believe it is so crucial to understand Ephesians 4:27 if we are going to live lives of victory and power over sin and Satan. Paul indicates in this verse that if we harbor and nurture our sin, we give the devil a "place" in our lives. This word has the idea of a "foothold," a "place to stand," or "ground" in our hearts that he now occupies.

Once we have surrendered this ground to Satan, it's vitally important that we know how to take it back, to reclaim it, and then how to resist the tempter successfully by using the spiritual armor God provides for us (Ephesians 6:10–18).

This is the crux, the heart, of spiritual warfare. I believe the concepts I have just outlined are so indispensable to waging successful war against Satan that I am happy to recommend James Logan's book to you.

Dr. Logan is a veteran of many years in the battle, and he has helped thousands of people to find new freedom and lasting victory in Christ. His book shows step by step how you or someone you love can reclaim the ground the enemy has gained in your life, even if Satan is well-entrenched on that ground inside his strongholds. The weapons Christ gives us are able to tear down Satan's strongholds and replace them with fortresses of truth. *Reclaiming Surrendered Ground* is a much-needed book, and I pray that God will open your spiritual eyes and ears to His truth as you read.

CHARLES STANLEY
Pastor, First Baptist Church of Atlanta

ACKNOWLEDGMENTS

In preparing this manuscript, I gratefully acknowledge Mark Ellis for his help with Greek words, Stan Udd for his help with Hebrew words, and Bill Gothard, for the significant work he and his staff at the Institute in Basic Life Principles have done in the areas of taking back ground and tearing down strongholds in the lives of hundreds of families.

I am especially grateful to Phil Rawley, who put this book into logical order and helped me express well important ideas. Without him, there would be no book.

Dennis Shere and Moody Press believed *Reclaiming Surrendered Ground* would help people find inner freedom, and I thank him for believing in me and the need for this book. To Jim Vincent, my editor, I say thank you for your careful checking of the manuscript for clarity and accuracy.

Finally, I am grateful to everyone at the International Center for Biblical Counseling for their encouragement throughout the project and as daily co-servants in ministry.

INTRODUCTION

The first recorded attack of Satan was upon the family, and as the twentieth century comes to a close, Satan is still attacking the family. The fall and spiritual defeat of Adam and Eve had both immediate consequences for them and their children, and far-reaching consequences that are still being felt today. Satan continues to use every means at his disposal, and the Christian family seems to be one of his main targets.

Though his ultimate defeat is assured, and his power over the Christian is limited, Satan still can influence followers of Jesus toward sin. He is looking for a "place," the apostle Paul tells us in Ephesians 4:27, an opportunity to gain a foothold in the family using any family member possible. Once he has gained his foothold, Satan sets about to work ruin in that family. This book is about protecting your family against such attacks and reclaiming any ground Satan may have in your life.

Another word for the *place, opportunity,* or *foothold* that Satan seeks to gain in our lives is *ground,* which is the idea behind the Greek word Paul used. Thus, throughout this book we will talk about what it means to "give ground" to the enemy; that is, to permit him to exercise influence over us by the sins and wrong behavior patterns we allow in our lives.

Ephesians 4:27 makes it clear that the believer is the one who yields this ground to Satan. He has no authority in a Christian's life except that which the Christian surrenders to him.

Pastor and author Warren Wiersbe explains what it means to give ground to Satan:

> If the believer cultivates in his life any known sin, he is giving Satan an opportunity to get a foothold, a beachhead in his life. Satan will then use this opportunity to invade and take over other areas. Paul warns in Ephesians 4:27, "And do not give the devil an

opportunity." The word translated "opportunity" simply means a place, such as a city or a building. But it carries the idea of a foothold or opportunity, a chance to operate."[1]

If it is possible for a believer to give ground to the enemy, then it is possible—in fact, it is crucial—for that believer, in the power of the Holy Spirit, to take back the ground he or she has yielded to the enemy.

This is the heart of the book. I want to help you understand the different ways that God's people can give ground to Satan. But most important, I want to guide you and your family, by our study of God's Word and by specific steps of action you can take, to regain any ground that has been surrendered to Satan. Beginning with chapter 3, you will find in each chapter a one-page list of practical steps, called "Higher Ground," that will help you and your family remove satanic influence in your lives. The fourteen "Higher Grounds" have proven effective in the counseling ministry of the International Center for Biblical Counseling (ICBC) in Sioux City, Iowa, of which I am a member.

When Moody Press first approached me about writing a book, I declined. I am not a writer, my counseling load is extremely heavy, and there are numerous books in print on various aspects of spiritual warfare.

But as I dealt with people over the phone, at conferences, and in my office, and realized the havoc Satan is wreaking in Christian families, I felt a book on biblical truths I have found in God's Word and confirmed in my spiritual counseling could help families.

A little about myself. I have been doing what I call "spiritual warfare counseling" with Christians for more than ten years. I assure you this wasn't a ministry I went looking for. I am super-conservative in my theology. My background is classic evangelicalism all the way, meaning that I was taught and believed that while demons and the demonic world were real, they really didn't manifest themselves in any significant way in the daily lives of God's people. That was just a little too radical a thought.

In fact, full-time involvement in teaching and counseling on the topic of spiritual warfare is foreign to everything I was trained for, and everything I taught myself as a Bible college professor, chaplain, and then as the pastor of four conservative churches over a period of twenty years. But while counseling missionaries with a major evangelical mission, I had to help a Christian woman clearly under satanic attack. My experience with this missionary, recounted in chapter 1, changed my thinking about satanic influence on Christians and brought me into warfare counseling. Since then I have counseled hundreds of families where satanic influence clearly is present.

I have seen it proved true countless numbers of times: when one family member is being defeated by the enemy, it can have devastating effects upon the whole family. A teenager in rebellion, a father in some form of spiritual bondage, or a mother who is hurting will affect the entire family. The enemy knows this. That's why he's working so hard to gain a foothold in your family and mine!

In laying out the book it seemed logical to start with the issues that could apply to any member of the family, then move to the specific relationships within the family. The testimonies used in the book have been slightly altered where necessary to protect the identity of the families involved. The names of all counselees mentioned have been changed as part of this protection.

Many of the personal testimonies you will read in this book have been taken from the prayer letters I send periodically to my ministry supporters. Almost without exception, the testimonies were written by the counselees themselves.

The counseling center of which I am a part is a nonprofit organization dedicated to helping people live in the spiritual victory that Christ won for us on the cross. My counselees come from all across the country, and on occasion from foreign countries, for a week of intensive counseling.

The heart of our ministry is helping people discover where they have given ground to the enemy, and leading them to reclaim that ground and come to the full inner freedom which is every Christian's birthright in Christ. The procedure I follow is set forth in this book.

We make no charge for our counseling services. Instead, we look to God to meet our needs, just as a missionary does. How thankful we are for the churches and individuals who stand with us through their prayers and financial gifts.

The ministry of warfare counseling has attracted wide international interest. Mark Bubeck, president of ICBC, also directs our biannual conference attended by representatives from counseling ministries all over the United States and many foreign countries. About six hundred people gather at these conferences to hear speakers selected from Bible colleges and seminaries and professional counselors chosen for their expertise in spiritual warfare and how it relates to the counseling profession.

The fact is that Satan desires to put so much pressure on your family that you will give up without a fight. But Ephesians 6 tells us that when we have done everything we can to stand, to keep on standing. I trust this book will help you to do just that. The victory is yours in Jesus Christ! If there are specific areas of struggle in your own life or in your family that you need additional help with, contact our ICBC office and we will do all we can to help you.

—Part 1—

Becoming Alert
to the Battle

—1—
THE BATTLE
AND THE VICTORY

If you knew a thief was planning to break into your home tonight, what would you do? At the very least, you would probably turn on every light inside and outside, and sit up to watch for his coming so you could thwart his plans. That's wise prevention. This is what I want to do in this book—help to forewarn and prepare you to protect your family from the enemy.

This is a book about spiritual warfare, an issue that affects every reader, Christian and non-Christian. Spiritual battles also involve the family, as the book's subtitle reveals. The fact is that Satan, our great enemy, has a well-focused plan of attack against families—husbands, fathers, wives, mothers, and children. Unless we know what he's up to, we cannot protect ourselves against his schemes.

You may be questioning some of these statements. *Well, spiritual warfare may have been an issue during the days of John Bunyan and* The Pilgrim's Progress, *and it's a problem today in primitive cultures, where animism and witchcraft prevail. But it's not a problem that my family or I will face.* You are not alone in thinking that way. Many evangelical Christians and most Americans relegate the topic of spiritual warfare to the old days. "Back in the Middle and Dark Ages, people weren't as enlightened as they are now," they argue. "We know so much more than those people did, so we don't have to ascribe a supernatural explanation to many of the things that happen to us. Modern science and the principles of psychology can account for many of the things our ancestors thought were supernatural."

Even more Americans believe that spirits are only active in more primitive countries. Here animism rules: people believe that God left His spirits to run the world. Though they don't worry about the good spirits, animistic people spend their whole lives in mortal fear of offending wicked spirits. Americans believe they struggle with real or imagined spiritual enemies because of their openness to them.

Christians rightly reject the animistic view of the world. But while Christians in the Western world believe in the supernatural, many still believe that everything on earth can be accounted for either by natural or scientific explanations. I've met numbers of Christians who don't really believe that the spirit world is real or relevant or needs to be dealt with.

People don't often come out and say that, but they reveal it by the way they react. As Timothy Warner, professor emeritus at Trinity Evangelical Divinity School and a board member at the International Center for Biblical Counseling, an agency that counsels people suspected of having problems with demonic influences, says, "People may not always live what they profess, but they will always live what they believe."

The Reality of Spiritual Warfare

Your profession level of belief probably is a theoretical or theological statement of dogma; it agrees with your religion. But your true belief is revealed by what you do under pressure. Most of us, during times of pressure, will not consider that a spiritual battle may be underway in our lives.

But we are often in a fierce battle with the enemy of our souls. Spiritual warfare is a biblical reality. The question is not whether we wrestle demonic spirits, but who's on top? Do the spirits have us pinned?

Members of Christian families, and sometimes entire families, are being wiped out left and right. It's not because they don't have the power or resources for victory, but because many of God's people don't take the enemy and his work seriously, much less recognize his attacks and try to resist him. The apostle Paul said he didn't want the Corinthian believers to be ignorant of Satan's devices (2 Corinthians 2:11), but the church of Jesus Christ today is woefully ignorant of the way our enemy works.

A Daily Battle

Please understand that I am not talking about bizarre happenings or things flying through the air. I have seen visible manifestations of demons in my counseling experience, but these are far from the norm. When these things do occur, I'm usually dealing with people who are so heavily in bondage to the enemy in one way or another that he has an enormous amount of ground to operate in their lives.

For the vast majority of Christians, however, spiritual warfare is another name for the daily battle we wage against "all that is in the world, the lust of the flesh, and the lust of the eyes, and the pride of life" (1 John 2:16).

Even though most of us memorized verses like this when we were children, we still don't understand how Satan works. The church is paying an enormous price for this neglect and ignorance of one of the central truths of the Christian life, the fact that spiritual warfare is real and we are in a battle.

Three in Battle

That's why I thought it would be helpful right up front to give you some insight into the seriousness of the battle by introducing you to three people whom I have met and counseled during the past few years.

Mary, Angie, and Bill are very different people in very different circumstances. But they have two things in common. First, they are sincere, everyday Christians, members of Christian families who could be your neighbors or fellow church members. Second, each of them has come face-to-face with the reality of spiritual warfare and has seen how the battle can affect individual believers and their families.

Mary is in her early fifties, rearing two children with her husband, Rob. Rob is a respected member of his community and a lay leader in their church; yet in recent years he has become harsh toward her and rejected her every effort to express love and concern.

Mary didn't know it at first, but her husband was fighting a losing battle against a particular problem in his own life. His repeated episodes of spiritual defeat had given Satan all the opening he needed to bring destructive temptations into this man's life. And because Mary's husband was not living in isolation, his struggle affected those closest to him.

Mary soon realized that her situation was not just a momentary setback and that Rob's battle was more than a flesh-and-blood struggle. She knew she had a decision to make: whether to give up on the marriage altogether, or stay but surrender to the bitterness and anger, which would give the enemy an opening into her life too.

Thankfully, Mary chose a third option, and God gave her the strength to carry it out. Here is part of the testimony she wrote and gave to me:

> This is a testimony to the love and faithfulness of God, who used a very lonely and difficult time in my marriage to draw me to Himself in a deep and intimate way. . . .
>
> Five years passed from the time I first suspected demonic involvement in my husband's life until his deliverance. As I had learned more and more about spiritual warfare, I realized that the heavy and dark spirit that sometimes characterized him was not necessary. He would sometimes take days of prayer and fasting, but with no joy. He was burdened with thoughts he didn't want to have but could not get

rid of. He was cold, rejecting and critical of me most of the time, and I really think he felt badly about that but could not rise above it.

One prayer I prayed during these five years was that if my husband needed deliverance, the Lord Jesus would bring it about in His time and His way. The situation was in His hands, and I knew I must leave it there. I was learning in a special way that I can always trust the Lord Jesus to do what is right and good, even if I don't understand how He is going to accomplish it.

I came to the point where I could tell the Lord that for my husband's sake I would like to see him set free, but for my sake it was all right if nothing ever changed because Jesus Himself was enough.

I am especially grateful that the Lord made it clear to me that He was not desirous of just an outward response of love [toward her husband], but that He was able to give me a heart response of love. That kept me from allowing bitterness in my own life. As a result, when my husband went to Jim Logan and was really set free, our relationship was restored in a beautiful way immediately.

It was a real answer to prayer when Mary's husband agreed to come for counseling. What a thrill it was for me to see him come to true freedom in Christ as I presented to him the very same truths I will share with you in this book.

In Angie's case, I knew the family very well and had dealt with one of her brothers who was having serious struggles of his own. In the course of my involvement with the family, I counseled Angie's father, a man who is thoroughly committed to the Lord, to pray that any hidden problems in the family would be brought to light.

None of us knew at the time that Angie, age sixteen, had been struggling with suicidal thoughts since she was a very young girl. For years she kept the thoughts to herself out of fear that her dad would be angry with her and reject her if she told him she was having these thoughts.

To all outward appearances, Angie was just a teenager who loved the Lord and was really serious about her Christian faith. She thought her problem was strictly a private struggle because she never hinted to anyone that she had it. "Ever since I was a very, very young child I had thought of how I could kill myself and the different ways I could do it." Angie later told me. "I even planned out my suicide note. It was a secret I decided I would never tell anyone."

But as Angie says in her own testimony that follows, when one family member allows himself or herself to come under demonic influence—and this was clearly the source of her destructive thoughts, as I'll point out later —it opens the way for the enemy to bring destructive attacks on the rest of the family.

Eventually God answered her father's prayers. After an incident that happened to Angie while she was on a youth missions trip, she told the leader about her secret problem. This godly man led her to freedom in Christ. Angie found release, and now has only one regret, that she had not come to her father earlier. In her testimony she wrote:

> I wish I had told my father about it a long time ago. When I told him he was understanding and helpful, not angry. I can see that it was the enemy influencing me to think my father would reject me because of my problem. Since I recognized the true source of these thoughts and renounced the enemy's influence, to this day I have not dwelt on or considered suicidal thoughts.
>
> I realize now how much ground I had given to Satan by allowing him to intrude these thoughts into my mind and cause me to become obsessed with them. I learned that when one family member [her brother] allows Satan's influence, this gives an open door to the enemy to bring destructive attacks on the rest of the family.

Angie is still free of these thoughts and living joyfully in the Lord. A detailed discussion of the enemy's strategy will come in the following chapters, so let me just note here that Angie's struggle was with what we call "intruding thoughts" from the enemy. As we will see, he does have access to our minds.

And by the way, lest you think Angie is unusual, far more teenagers and young children struggle with similar thoughts than most of us will ever imagine. My point is that she is a normal and lovely teen who fell prey to one of the enemy's favorite tactics. After all, we'll see later in this chapter that Satan's plan is to steal, kill, and destroy. He doesn't care how young his targets happen to be.

The third person I want to introduce to you is my friend Bill, who did actually try to take his own life on one occasion. Praise God the attempt failed, and Bill finally decided to seek help. Bill was a husband and father with a devoted wife and a houseful of lively children whom he loved dearly.

You might be saying to yourself, *Bill couldn't have loved his family very much if he tried to kill himself. Didn't he know that would only make things much worse?*

Bill did—and does—love his family very much, but the enemy had so twisted Bill's thinking that he actually believed his death would spare his family any more heartache.

What drove this talented and outwardly successful young husband, father, and sincere Christian to try and destroy himself? Bill was held by a particular form of sexual bondage that had a seeming death grip on his life. Bill's problems had begun very early, but his Christian parents never had any idea of his affliction. After Bill tried and failed to take his life, he sought Christian counseling. He spent a month in a psychiatric clinic under the treatment of one of the top Christian counseling ministries in the country. At the end of this time, he was told he was a helpless sex addict for whom there was no hope of cure. He would have to become part of an ongoing 12-step treatment program every week for the rest of his life.

By the time I was able to see Bill, he had spent a year-and-a-half, and thousands of dollars, on Christian counseling. He was in terrible shape. As we will see in later chapters, Bill's bondage also allowed the enemy to bring destructive attacks upon his family (Matthew 12:29).

The last time you will meet Bill in this book is when we discuss in detail the wonderful work God did in Bill's life and the lives of his wife and children when he dealt with the root causes of his problem. I'm telling you about him here, and about Mary and Angie, just to pull back the corner of the box lid, so to speak, to give you a preview of how satanic influence can affect families and individuals.

The effect of Satan's attacks on families can be devastating, particularly if he can get to the father as God's appointed authority and spiritual protector in the home. When a father yields to sin and opens his life to the enemy's temptation and control, he also clears the way for Satan to reach into his family and attack his children. Or, if he cannot get to Dad, the enemy will often attack the wife and mother, which also affects her husband and children. And if dad and mom are not buying his strategy, Satan is cruel enough to turn his fiery darts on the children.

But I want to say right here that he is a defeated foe! That's the good news God's Word has for you.

Welcome to the War

I have been doing what I call "warfare counseling" with Christians for more than ten years now. This is a ministry that has grown tremendously in recent years as more of God's people become alert to the fact that there's a war on.

My friend Neil Anderson, a former seminary professor and a bestselling author, has his own work called Freedom in Christ Ministries. I also work with the Institute in Basic Life Principles, which helps thousands of families each year. Besides ministries like these and our own Counseling Center, warfare counselors like myself and others are regularly invited to teach the principles of warfare at many mission agencies, denominational conferences, and parachurch ministries. We also speak to large audiences of parents, children and pastors.

Of course, I know now that we are not the first generation to learn the truth about spiritual warfare. One of the 400-plus warfare books in my library is a work entitled *Precious Remedies Against Satan's Devices,* written in 1652 by Thomas Brooks! It's one of many classics on warfare written long ago, and they are as up-to-date as today's newspaper when it comes to the principles of warfare. Two later classics are *War on the Saints*, by Jessie Penn-Lewis, and *Demon Possession*, by John L. Nevis.

A Doubter

I must admit, though, that I was not initially a believer in demonic attacks on Christians. Like many evangelicals, I rejected the idea that demons could have any kind of influence on God's people. My unbelief was not at the theological level, of course. Theologically, I acknowledged the existence of evil spirits. I had to, because the Bible taught about them, and I was—and still am—a thoroughgoing biblicist. That is, I accept the Bible as God's inerrant, infallible Word. But as far as the enemy's active work in the world, I pretty much relegated that to the two realms I mentioned above: either the "old days" or in primitive, spiritually backward countries.

For all I knew, nothing would be different in that area when I joined the ministry of a major evangelical mission in 1982. This was, and still is, one of the largest mission agencies in the world, with missionaries in more than one hundred countries. I was an assistant to the president, ministering to and counseling missionaries around the world. It was here that God began to open my eyes to the reality of spiritual warfare.

One day during that time a missionary came to me and said, "Jim, there's something wrong with my partner. I think she has a demonic problem."

Becoming a Believer

I can't tell you how stunned I was when she said that. These women were veteran missionaries who had impacted the world for Christ. The missionary this woman was talking about had forty years of experience on the field. So I said to this missionary who was concerned about her partner, "No, she doesn't. That's impossible."

"Well, impossible or not, you better call her in, because you're the counselor of the mission."

I didn't want to call this woman in either way, because what if it were true? I wouldn't know what to do. I had no training or background to deal with something like this. As I said, I only believed in demons because the Bible talked about them.

Of course, as the counselor for the mission, I made arrangements to see this career missionary. When she finally entered my office, I knew something was seriously wrong. I understand now that she came under a demonic attack.

Her behavior was bizarre. She would spout religious cliches, for example. The demons were mocking me and my feeble attempts to help her. Much later I realized that she had religious spirits, although of course I didn't know it at the time.

I believe these are spirits like those Paul mentions in 1 Timothy 4:1, whose particular assignment is to deceive people with false religious ideas rather than enticements to evil acts. The effect, though, is the same: deception and eventual bondage.

In my years of counseling I've found that these are the most deceptive spirits. This dear lady wasn't doing anything outwardly wicked. On the contrary, she seemed to be incredibly pious. But something was out of whack. She scared me, to be honest. Her body was there at the mission headquarters, but she, the person inside, was completely out of control.

I learned later that she was an illegitimate child who was adopted by her family. We'll talk more about this later in relation to the work of the enemy, because a person's background is very important in this area. We'll see how iniquities are passed on generationally and how this gives the enemy an advantage in bringing destructive attacks on the family (Exodus 20:5).

I'm convinced this woman's spirits were ancestral, an "inheritance" from her birth family. She had a whole notebook full of insights the demons had given her.

I couldn't do anything to help her, so I called a man who is a highly respected theologian and very knowledgeable in this area. I felt desperate by now.

We sent our missionary to see him, but he couldn't help her either. In fact, she wound up in a mental hospital for four days in a straitjacket. It really bothers me to think about what she had to go through—most of it needlessly. But she finally came to full freedom, and has a wonderful testimony of how God set her free. Today, she is still impacting the world for Christ.

Understanding the Battle

That eye-opening and scary incident was my introduction to the reality of spiritual warfare. It suggested to me that any Christian, even a missionary or pastor, could be open to satanic influences. I began to wonder if I had missed something in all my years of Bible study, teaching, and preaching. I realized I needed to go back and read what the Bible has to say about demons.

My re-education began with reading the entire New Testament and marking every verse that dealt with spiritual warfare. Then I did Greek word studies on each of those verses and counseled with godly New Testament professors and theologians to make sure I had a handle on the verses. Since then I've gone through the New Testament many, many times, and the Old Testament as well. I've also read more than four hundred books on spiritual warfare over the past ten years, and I still re-read some of the classic works regularly.

This book is the fruit of these years of study and ministry. Along the way you will also read the testimonies of a number of believers: Christians of all ages and from all walks of life whose lives were thrown in the ditch spiritually by demonic attacks because they did not understand the vital truths about our enemy, our identity, and our armor.

Our Enemy

1. The enemy is strong. This is the first vital truth. A battle is underway for the hearts, minds, and even lives, of God's people. Satan is the enemy, and he and his followers have a definite strategy to come against us and defeat us. "Your adversary the devil, as a roaring lion, walketh about, seeking whom he may devour" (1 Peter 5:8).

I put it this way to the people I teach and counsel: Satan hates you and has a terrible plan for your life. Unlike the good news of God's love, Satan's plan is to steal, kill, and destroy (John 10:10).

First, he wants to steal the eternal significance of your life. He wants to get you so wrapped up in your problems and circumstances that you never reach out to others. That way, you're no threat to him at all. Satan wants to steal the fruit of the Spirit in your life. That's why every attack of the enemy is designed to get your eyes off of Christ (Hebrews 12:2) and onto yourself and your problems.

Second, Satan desires to kill you. But he can't do that without God's permission, so he'll tell you to do it for him. Most of the people I deal with have had serious thoughts of suicide because like Bill, they're convinced it's the only way out.

I might as well end it all, they reason. Others think, *My situation is hopeless; I might as well give up and divorce my wife.* And some believe, *Oh, I'm just born that way. I've got bad genes, or a physical problem.* Each abandons hope he or she can be useful to God; they move to the sidelines as injured servants of God.

Third, the enemy seeks to destroy our relationships. Churches and pastors are being shredded by the enemy's work in tearing apart relationships.

But Satan is a toothless lion. He was stripped of his power at the cross of Jesus Christ (see Colossians 2:15). So in 1 Peter 5, the apostle goes on to say, "Whom resist stedfast in the faith" (v. 9).

If this is true, why do we see all of this happening? Because we have been delivered from the power, not the presence, of darkness (Colossians 1:13). The whole world lies in the lap of the wicked one (1 John 5:19). Since Satan is defeated, his power is in the lie. I'll have a lot more to say about that later.

Our Identity

2. *Our spiritual identity as children of God gives us the authority and power to repel the enemy's attacks.* We are to be "more than conquerors through him that loved us" (Romans 8:37). In the following chapters, we'll see who we are in Christ, primarily from the book of Ephesians.

Our Armor

3. *God gives us mighty armor to resist the enemy's attacks.* We need to "put on the whole armour of God" (Ephesians 6:11) to resist Satan successfully.

I speak regularly at conferences around the country and overseas. No matter the audience—missionaries, pastors, or parents and their children—I find that every child of God is a target of Satan's attacks. But I also find the armor of God is sufficient for every person's battle. The armor, consisting of truth, righteousness and much more (Ephesians 6:10–18), is the only way to resist Satan's attacks. And it is, thank God, the effective way.

Waging Successful Warfare

The good news is that not every believer falls prey to these attacks in the way Bill did. There are believers, young and old, across this country and around the world who have been trained and equipped from Scripture to deal successfully with this area of the Christian life. And many of these people are helping other believers who have fallen victim to the enemy and are being held in various degrees of bondage.

Being Aware

That's why I have attempted to write a book that will be helpful to readers like you on several levels. First, I want to make you aware of the spiritual battle going on around you and equip you to wage it successfully.

As I said, every believer is subject to Satan's schemes. But if you don't know the source of the thoughts and temptations that you encounter each day, you can be tripped up and eventually wiped out.

For example, what would happen if you really believed that every single wrong thought which enters your mind originated from you? Worse yet, what if you believed that because it was your thought, you had to welcome it, entertain it, and act on it? You'd be a mess, to put it simply.

You say, "That's ridiculous. I know that I don't have to accept and act out every thought that enters my head." You're right. But that's exactly what the enemy has convinced some Christians to believe and to do, and it's destroying them.

Being Equipped

So my first purpose is to alert you that there's a battle going on. My second purpose is to help equip you to fight the good fight of faith, to stand in the victory Christ has provided. You see, I don't ask people, "Do you have the victory?" That's the wrong question. What we need to ask is, "Are you standing in the victory you already have in Christ?"

Helping Others

A third purpose is to help you deal with someone else who is coming under demonic attack. Angie's father had already been trained in warfare ministry and prayer and was active in his role as spiritual protector of his family when her problem was brought to light and dealt with.

Many of my counselees have gone home from my office and led their wives, husbands, or children through the steps to freedom I will share with you in these pages. I believe you will find that the principles in this book are usable with your own family and can easily be taught to others.

The methods and Scriptures I use in my counseling—which, by the way, is a week-long process—are neither mysterious nor magical. Thousands of pastors, missionaries, and lay people have been trained to recognize the signs of demonic involvement and lead someone to freedom in Christ.

You could say I'm trying to work myself out of a job. By the time a person calls our office for an appointment and travels across the country or even from overseas to spend a week in Sioux City in intense biblical counseling, that person is in pretty bad shape. We receive 5,000 calls a year from all over the world. Sometimes our secretaries can hardly handle the phone calls, they are so tragic.

But no believer in Jesus Christ needs to get to that critical stage. Since spiritual warfare is every Christian's common experience, God has equipped every believer with every spiritual weapon necessary to fight a winning battle. The following chapters will show you how.

The first thing we'll do in chapter 2, however, is deal with an important question which, if it hasn't already occurred to you, will come up very soon.

— 2 —
GIVING AND GAINING SPIRITUAL GROUND

Whenever I teach on the subject of spiritual warfare or counsel a person in my office, I try to deal with a very important and valid question. Maybe it has already occurred to you. The question is this: can a Christian be demon-possessed? Put another way, can the Holy Spirit and an evil spirit occupy the same territory in a person's life?

Depending on how you answer that question, you probably will or will not believe that demonic influence and attacks on a Christian are even a possibility. Many people come to this issue with a pretty firm idea of what they believe. But some of the conclusions we draw are more on the order of inferences rather than interpretations of direct biblical teaching.

Defining Terms

The issue of the Christian and demonic activity is a hot button. But that doesn't mean we can ignore it or retreat to the safety of the standard answers. My friend and fellow warfare counselor Neil Anderson says, "No question polarizes the Christian community more than this one, and the tragedy is that there is no absolutely biblical way to answer it."[1]

"Possession"

What Anderson means is that the New Testament does not directly answer the question of whether a Christian can be demon-possessed. That's because the New Testament doesn't really address the issue of demon possession, as we commonly think of it, in relation to the Christian.

In fact, the very term *demon possession* itself is part of the problem. It is used in most English versions of the Bible to translate a single Greek word—and it may not be the best translation at all. Tim Warner says,

The use of the word "possession" to translate the expressions used in the Greek New Testament to indicate the relationship between demons and people is unfortunate, if not unwarranted. We obtained our English word "demon" by transliterating the Greek word *daimon*. We should have done the same with the Greek word *daimonizomai*—a verb form of the same Greek root. It would then come into English as "demonize" and we could then speak of the degree to which a person could be demonized rather than being limited to the either-or options imposed by the possessed-not possessed view.[2]

I believe Warner is on target when he concludes, "Spiritual 'possession' clearly implies ownership and would seem to include the control of one's eternal destiny. [It] would be impossible to be owned and controlled by Satan and have a saving relationship with Christ at the same time. So if the question is, 'Can a Christian be demon-possessed?', the answer is clearly no."[3]

A Continuum

Warner's conclusion is an inference from the Scriptures; we cannot point to a specific chapter and verse. But I think it's the right inference. We who know Christ have been bought by Him at the cost of His blood. And I don't see any place in the Bible where Christ sells me to the devil.

However, as Warner indicates above, the issue of Satan's work in a Christian's life is not a stark, either/or choice of no influence or full possession. It is better represented by a continuum, ranging from mere suggestion to what I would call a dominating and destructive influence. Neil Anderson observes,

> The fact that a Christian can be influenced to one degree or another by the "god of this world" is a New Testament given. If not, then why are we instructed to put on the armor of God and stand firm (Eph. 6:10), to take every thought captive to the obedience of Christ (2 Cor. 10:5), and to resist the devil (James 4:7)? And what if we don't put on the armor of God, stand firm, assume responsibility for what we think; and what if we fail to resist the devil? Then what? We are easy prey for the enemy of our souls.[4]

We've already looked at 1 Peter 5:8. What does it mean to be devoured by Satan? Why does God warn me of that if it's not a possibility? The word *devour* means "to gobble down quickly." Satan not only wants to eat your lunch, he wants to eat you! Warner spells out so clearly the tremendous damage Satan is doing to the body of Christ because so many refuse to recognize his influence:

Only eternity will reveal the number of believers who have led unproductive, frustrated lives and of Christian workers who have been forced to forsake their ministries because of attacks of the enemy. This happens in spite of the fact that the New Testament warnings concerning demonic activity are all addressed to believers. . . . How RESIST got changed to IGNORE in so many segments of the Church, I don't know. When it did, however, Satan and his forces gained a great strategic advantage.[5]

"Influence"

The key word in everything that has been said to this point, at least for believers, is *influence.* When it comes to God's people, evil spirits are spirits of influence only. That's not true for unbelievers in the world. They are held firmly in Satan's grasp, under his control, blinded in their hearts and minds and utterly dead to spiritual truth until quickened by the Holy Spirit. They are members of his kingdom of darkness (Ephesians 2:2).

But as we've seen, Christians are already "possessed" (owned) by the Holy Spirit, so demonic possession in the sense of ownership is not the issue. Rather, the issue is the influence the evil one can exert on us. "In discussing demonic spiritual warfare on the personal level," Scott Moreau explains, "one general principle must be noted at the onset: demons can only influence believers to the extent that we allow them to do so." Moreau, assistant professor of missions and intercultural studies at Wheaton Graduate School, adds, "The act of giving or allowing Satan to take any amount of control in our life is referred to as 'giving ground.'"[6]

Giving Ground to the Enemy

Moreau is referring to Paul's warning in Ephesians 4:27. After cautioning us not to let our anger simmer overnight, Paul says, "Neither give place to the devil." The word translated *place* here is the Greek word *topos.* This word might look familiar to you even in its original form. It's at the root of English words like topography, and refers to the ground or a specific spot or location.

So giving place to Satan in our lives is giving him ground, a "foothold" according to the *New International Version* of the Bible, an "opportunity" (NASB and *Revised Standard Version*), a "chance" (*Today's English Version*). On the other side, one commentator describes Paul's admonition as allowing the devil "no leeway . . . no room to move."[7]

Gaining Entrance

All of these translations, and there are others, add up to a very graphic description of the way Satan can gain entrance into a believer's life. Clinton Arnold, associate professor of New Testament at the Talbot School of Theology, describes the process and how to resist this way:

> It is likely that any sinful activity that the believer does not deal with by the power of the Spirit can be exploited by the devil and turned into a means of control over a believer's life. Therefore, Christians need to resist. For Paul there is no middle ground. There is no nominal Christianity. Believers either resist the influence of the evil one who works through the flesh and the world, or they relinquish control of their lives to the power of darkness. Giving in to those temptations does not just confirm the weakness of the flesh, it opens up the lives of believers to the control of the devil and his powers. We need to recognize the supernatural nature of temptation and be prepared to face it.[8]

Ephesians 4:26 is the immediate context of Paul's warning and a wonderful example of how we can give spiritual ground to Satan. This verse clearly allows for proper anger. That is beyond dispute. But what happens when anger simmers unchecked in our soul? It degenerates into bitterness—a sin that gives Satan an opening into our lives big enough to drive a truck through! (See chapter 4 for an in-depth treatment of the crucial topic of bitterness.)

Building Strongholds

Why would Satan want to gain ground, a foothold, in our hearts? It gives him a beachhead from which to attack us with destructive temptations. He uses this ground to build his "strongholds" of lies and thereby begins to undercut our relationship with and testimony for Jesus. Ed Silvoso, an Argentine who directs an international evangelistic work called Harvest Ministries, aptly defines a satanic stronghold: "A stronghold is a mindset impregnated with hopelessness that causes me to accept as unchangeable something that we know is contrary to the will of God."[9]

On first reading, that definition might sound a little complex. But it's really very simple, and very powerful. Remember Bill? In his struggle with a sexual sin he eventually became convinced he was a woman trapped in a man's body and could never change. (His mind was "impregnated with hopelessness.") He was so convinced that he decided to commit suicide.

What did Bill's mindset say about God? It said that God made a huge mistake. He "wired" Bill wrong. Something got confused. God meant for me to be a woman, but He put me in a man's body, Bill told himself. *So He's either an incompetent Creator or very cruel.*

Imagine all of that going through the mind of a Christian—and being believed. That's a stronghold! These patterns of thought get burned into our minds either over a period of time or by traumatic experiences. Then they come out in unchristian attitudes and behaviors that are often either not recognized, or if recognized, seldom seen as choices.

When this happens you hear people say things like, "I may be an angry person, but I can't help it. That's the way God made me."

Pastor Jackson once told his congregation, "I'm an angry man. You'll just have to learn to live with me." After five-and-one-half years, the members couldn't take it anymore, and he was asked to leave. Later a divisive church split occurred. Though the pastor's anger may not be the sole cause of the split, the tensions he created and his subsequent departure probably created the division among the flock.

Satan's Pawns?

This concept of giving ground to the enemy is so critical that I build my counseling on it. Notice that we as believers can give ground to Satan. He can't take it without our cooperation and permission. All he can do is influence us: plant evil thoughts, make suggestions, place temptations in our path.

I want to keep coming back to this idea of influence because it is so important to waging successful spiritual warfare. No Christian is a helpless pawn of Satan! That's why we don't ever want to become fixated on the enemy and his power. Our focus is to be on Christ (Hebrews 12:1–2).

You might say, "It's odd that you say you don't want me to concentrate on Satan and his ways, since you're writing a book on that very subject."

That's true. But knowing how the enemy operates and becoming obsessed with him are two very different things. As I said earlier, most evangelicals err on the side of knowing far too little, not too much. A friend of mine has a great answer for those who accuse us in this ministry of "seeing demons behind every bush." He replies, "My concern is that we see the bushes!"

You see, my greatest problem is not Satan, but myself. If I desire and decide to hold on to sin, I give the enemy the ground he needs to launch his destructive attacks against me. If I cherish sin in my life, Satan will seek to exploit it. Since I must serve someone (see Joshua 24:15), the fact is that any area of my life I don't yield to the Holy Spirit's control, Satan will control.

Legal Jurisdiction

It's helpful to think of "ground" as legal jurisdiction. When I give ground to Satan, I am giving him legal permission to attack me. As I indicated above, the enemy wants this ground so he can build strongholds on it. If Satan gets a firm enough foothold in a person's life, he can turn an act of sin into a regular practice of sin, and from there it degenerates into a habit which leads that person downward into bondage, where he "shall be holden with the cords of his sins" (Proverbs 5:22).

This downward spiral is fairly easy to discern in any form of bondage that has a physical component. For instance, most alcoholics didn't start by announcing, "I plan to ruin my life and my family by drinking as much alcohol as I can hold every day from here on out." No, it begins with a drink, then two, then a couple to get the person going in the morning and a couple more to help him unwind after a hard day. The slide downward can be traced from the initial act to a regular practice to a habit to bondage.

Addiction, or Sin?

By the way, I don't like to use the word *addiction* in my counseling. Addiction is a secular concept, and I don't like it because it suggests that I am a powerless victim of my problem. God calls it sin; the world calls it "bad genes."

We've got to choose which one we believe. If it's sin, there's hope. But if I'm just born this way, or if I'm just a helpless victim of some powerful force or substance, then my situation is hopeless. The issue is sin, and we can change. As I tell my counselees, the only "bad genes" are at your local discount department store!

Nurturing Sin

This is a good place to stop and make sure you understand what I am not saying. I am not saying that every single time we sin, we give Satan a huge chunk of ground on which he can build a towering stronghold. Can you imagine what a mess we would be if every sin we committed led to a satanic stronghold? Instead, we give ground when we refuse to let go of our sin, to confess it, and turn from it. I think that's very clear from Ephesians 4:26–27. It's not necessarily one moment of anger that gives Satan a foothold, but anger that is stored up, nurtured, and allowed to turn to bitterness and other horrible things the apostle goes on to describe in the closing verses of Ephesians 4.

In other words, giving ground and allowing Satan to build a stronghold on that ground are different issues. Giving ground is the enemy's entry point into our lives. Strongholds are belief systems that take more time and involvement to build.

As I said above, I believe that ground is yielded to the enemy when we cling to our sin rather than confess it and turn from it. Then if we persist in our sin, Satan has the time and opportunity he needs to build a stronghold on the ground he has taken from us.

I'm convinced that a satanic stronghold has been erected and is firmly in place in our lives by the time sin reaches the habit stage, if not before. You have to listen to and believe a whole lot of lies before Satan can get this kind of stranglehold on your life.

It may help to think of it this way. Giving ground is like giving Satan the land and the "building permit," the permission he needs to erect his stronghold. All he has to do then is start digging the foundation.

Believing Lies

The deception aspect of this is important to understand, because Ed Silvoso's definition of a stronghold makes it clear that satanic strongholds are built on a foundation of lies. The very "bricks" or foundation of a stronghold are lies. We know that Satan "is a liar, and the father of it" (John 8:44). Satan knows that if he can get our eyes off of Christ and on to our circumstances and problems, we'll soon be tripped up.

My son Richard was a cross-country runner during his teen years and through college. Now he runs for the fun of it. As a runner, he does two important things. First, he sets his focus on the finish line ahead of him. Second, he glances at the road ahead of him occasionally to watch for obstacles. If he were to focus on his feet, he would soon stumble and lose the race.

Lies can only trip us up if we believe them, of course. But once we believe Satan's lies, they become the truth for us. One lie I believed for years was that I was inferior, that I couldn't do anything right. My father was very critical, constantly criticizing me. He liked to tell me things I did were "stupid" and even said I was "dumb." My teenage years were a miserable time for me. I even tried to take my life when I was fifteen. When I failed, I remember thinking my dad must be right about me. I couldn't even kill myself.

I came to Christ at the age of nineteen, but that stronghold stayed in my life for years after that. I believed Satan's lie that I had little worth, and I lived in abject fear of rejection by people. Things got so bad that I couldn't even speak to groups. Here I was, a pastor, and I would almost get sick when I had to do a funeral, for example. My thoughts were always the same: What if the people didn't like what I had to say? What if they rejected me?

Years later, God helped me tear down that stronghold of the enemy's lies. Sitting in my office at the mission where I was a vice-president, I began to look back on my ministry. I realized that God had used my life. The thought occurred to me, *You're not dumb. If you were so dumb, you wouldn't be sitting where you're sitting.*

God reminded me of the truth that I was His child, special in His sight, chosen to serve Him with the gifts He gave. I was so excited by this thought that I wanted to run up and down the hall saying, "Hey, guess what, I'm not dumb!" The lie that I was dumb and worthless was a stronghold that had to come down. The truth that God could use me was a tower of truth I had to build in its place.

A Biblical Process

Now that I've used terms like "giving ground," "strongholds," and "towers of truth," let me show you where we're going with all of this. I lead my counselees through five biblical steps to freedom in Christ, and I want to present them now. These steps will be helpful to you both in leading someone else to freedom, and in equipping you and your family to wage successful spiritual warfare. Many people have discovered that because these principles are from the Word of God, the principles are effective for more than those who are in deep bondage to some habit or secret sin. They are also part of the "spiritual weapons" God has given all of us, weapons which are mighty through Him for "the pulling down of strong holds" (2 Corinthians 10:4).

I've seen God use the application of these simple principles to set men and women free from the most awful kind of spiritual bondage you can imagine.

I realize that some of the concepts I'm presenting may be new to you, so don't worry if everything doesn't fall into place right away. In a sense, I'm sharing the solution before I get deeply into the problem, but there's a reason for approaching things this way.

The five steps that follow (and the Scriptures that accompany them), will show up throughout the book. This overview will introduce you to important issues we will explore in depth as we go along. After I outline the steps that are at the heart of my ministry, we will look at some major problem areas that open our lives up to the influence and domination of Satan. Then we will finish the book with a strong affirmation of and detailed look at our identity in Christ, and the tremendous privileges and power that are ours in Him.

Steps to Freedom in Christ

In case I don't say it enough throughout the book, let me say it again right now: Satan is a defeated foe! He was rendered powerless at the cross of Jesus Christ. The enemy has no power over God's children except that power we permit him to have. Keep these thoughts in the forefront of your mind as we look at ways Satan can bring us under bondage and what it takes to defeat him.

1. Genuine Repentance

The first step in bringing anyone to genuine freedom in Christ is this: there must be *genuine repentance* of sin.

I once counseled a married couple trying to recover from an extramarital affair. The affair had many consequences, including the loss of work for this person's mate, which forced them to change locations. The new job did not pay much, which led to many financial problems and a lot of unhappiness. The partner who had the affair was crying profusely in my office as we talked about what had happened.

Assuming I knew why this person was crying, and wanting to be helpful, I said, "I understand why you're crying."

The response was, "No, I don't think you do. I'm crying because the affair is over."

I had assumed the tears were tears of repentance for the adultery. Not so! You cannot assume repentance on the part of another person. Conviction of sin is the Holy Spirit's work. Only He can put the finger on sin and bring the "godly sorrow [that] worketh repentance" (2 Corinthians 7:10).

Turning from sin includes confession and cleansing by the blood of Christ (1 John 1:9; 1 Peter 1:18–19), and a commitment to letting go of the sin. This has to be the first step, because without true repentance nothing of any lasting value will happen.

Scott, a Christian teen who was heavily into the occult, sought demonic powers in order to have a sense of power, of being in control. In his eyes, his powers were what set him apart from other kids and made him feel special. I told him that if he wanted to be free, he would have to renounce the work of the enemy in his life and commit himself to the Lord Jesus Christ. He didn't say anything, so I explained it again. Scott just looked at me.

So I started over, but he said "Stop. I know what you're saying. But if I give up my powers, I'll be just like everyone else."

"Yes, you will," I said—and he refused. Scott wasn't willing to give up the one thing that made him feel important, even though those same forces would try to destroy him. I told him he was free to go. There was nothing more I could do for him. Victory in spiritual warfare has to start with repentance.

2. Taking Back Ground

Step two in coming to freedom yourself or helping someone else find freedom is *taking back ground* that has been yielded to the enemy.

I've already laid out the biblical concept of yielding ground to Satan, so I won't repeat that here. How do I take back ground that has been surrendered to the enemy? By an open declaration to God that what I did was wrong.

This means verbally announcing that in the Lord's name and power, I am asking Him to take back any ground I have yielded to Satan. I announce to the forces of evil that here and now, I renounce Satan's works and ways in my life, that I want nothing to do with them anymore.

On the surface, this may sound like repentance. But I have found that taking back ground is a distinct step in helping a person come to true freedom in Christ. I ask the people I counsel to declare their intention out loud—and for many, this declaration is where the real battle starts.

Why? Because they are standing against Satan, in most cases for the very first time in their lives! These are Christians who have let Satan push them around and keep them in bondage their whole lives without ever once resisting him.

I have sat in my office with more than one sincere Christian who has told me, "I want to declare this, but I just can't. Something in my mind is telling me no. I can't get the words out." A pastor who I was counseling said, "Jim, I want to be sincere when I make my declaration. I don't just want to repeat words. But I can't do it." So I encouraged him to take a walk along the river and talk to the Lord about it. He did, then came back and came to true freedom.

Remember that "ground" is legal jurisdiction. It is like giving the enemy the key to my house. When I yield ground, I am giving the enemy permission to attack me with destructive thoughts and temptations. Looking at it from another angle, I have strayed into his jurisdiction, his territory, and that gives him a claim I must renounce.

This is why I said earlier that ground and strongholds are different issues. The occult (see chapter 3) is one area where we can clearly give Satan an advantage. Others include bitterness, unforgiveness, the lack of a clear conscience, pride, and sexual sin.

Once all ground has been taken back from the enemy (his legal right to attack me), this is the time to command the enemy in the name and blood of the Lord Jesus Christ to *leave* and go where Jesus sends him.

3. Tearing Down Strongholds

The third step in getting free of the enemy is *tearing down strongholds*. Remember, a stronghold is a fortress of lies Satan builds in your heart and mind. God wants us to tear down these structures, as we have seen (2 Corinthians 10:4). Unlike fortresses made of stone and brick, these strongholds can't be destroyed by the weapons of the flesh.

What undermines and destroys a lie? The truth! Jesus said it's truth that sets us free (John 8:32), but it is only when truth is believed and acted upon that it does the job.

Another reason we need to identify and tear down strongholds is because Satan is a deceiver (Revelation 12:9). That's one of his major attacks we have to deal with. A deception is when your mind and emotions believe something that isn't true. Deceptions may be 90 percent truth and only 10 percent lie, but the power of a deception is broken only when we recognize that it is a lie.

Satan is not only a liar and deceiver. He is also "the accuser of [the] brethren" (Revelation 12:10). This is his other major tactic. He will accuse God to me, me to God, and even me to me. He will intrude his thoughts into my mind, and then accuse me for having them. When I listened to my dad's assessment that I was dumb and worthless, for instance, I soon believed those words. It was a false belief, but those thoughts of inferiority became a real stronghold in my life.

Our belief systems are shaped by a number of significant forces: family, society, our peers, education, television, and even the music we listen to. That's why as believers we have to renew our minds (Romans 12:2) by thinking God's thoughts. One way we do this is by dwelling on those things that are honest, true, pure, lovely, and of "good report" (Philippians 4:8). I'll have more to say about this later.

4. Building Towers of Truth

As I like to tell my counselees, when you tear down a satanic stronghold, use the bricks to *build towers of truth*. This is the fourth step to freedom.

A tower of truth is just what the name implies: reprogramming your mind with the truth about yourself, about God, and about Satan and his ways. Then, when the enemy comes with his intruding thoughts —lies, deceptions, and accusations—you can flee to the tower.

Of course, God's Word is the ultimate source of the truth we need to replace Satan's strongholds of lies. In the Psalms, King David several times used this idea of a tower to which we can flee (see Psalm 18:1–3).

5. Taking Thoughts Captive

For this fifth and final step, we go back to 2 Corinthians 10, a critical passage that teaches us that the mind is the battleground between God and Satan in spiritual warfare.

Verse 5 instructs us to *take every thought captive* "to the obedience of Christ." We are to bring our thoughts in line with what He desires and what pleases Him.

Do you know what a wrong thought looks like? That is, would you recognize a wrong thought when you had one? You'd be surprised how many Christians don't. Or perhaps I should say, you'd be surprised by how many Christians think the horrible, vile, and even blasphemous thoughts Satan torments them with are actually their thoughts. What can you conclude about yourself if you believe these thoughts are coming from you? You'd have to conclude, "I must be a terrible, rotten person. No child of God would think like this. God can't love me when I have such wicked thoughts."

Many people who come to my office struggle terribly with intruding thoughts, often coming so fast they can't turn off the flow. I ask these people, "Are these terrible thoughts coming from God?"

The inevitable answer is "No, no way." But they cannot discern whether the thoughts are coming from them or from the enemy. Trying to deal with thoughts when they're coming that fast is exhausting. It's like a kid in a batting cage trying to hit with one hundred balls coming at him every minute. He's defenseless.

But Matthew 16:13–23 shows us that our thoughts can come from one of three sources: ourselves, God, and Satan. In verse 16, God put His thoughts into Peter's mind so that Peter spoke out the very mind of God when he confessed Jesus as the Son of God.

The interesting thing is that if Jesus hadn't told Peter this thought was from God, Peter wouldn't have known where it came from. He would have assumed it was his thought. But then in verse 22, Peter rebuked Jesus for talking about the cross. Jesus immediately informed Peter that this thought was from the devil.

These verses give us principles for walking in victory that are as important as any in the New Testament. Not all of the thoughts we have come from us. Woe to the person who cannot tell the difference between his own thoughts and those that come from Satan. God doesn't want us to be controlled by our thoughts. We are to control them (2 Corinthians 10:5).

In other words, don't let the enemy set your agenda. When the enemy sends an intruding thought, say "I give no consent to that," and move on. By the way, God hasn't left it up to us to decide what kinds of thoughts to shun and what kinds to embrace. Letting our minds dwell on the things described in Philippians 4:8 will help us discern when the enemy is attacking us with his intruding thoughts.

Now that we've set the goal toward which we want to move, let's talk about some of the ways that believers can give Satan ground in their lives.

— Part 2 —

Giving Ground, Reclaiming Ground

— 3 —
DABBLING IN DARKNESS

Nothing can throw an entire family into total distress faster than a teenage son or daughter having serious problems. If you have (or had) teenagers or know someone rearing teenagers, you know exactly what I'm talking about. In the area of the occult, our teens are falling into this trap of the enemy in record numbers. That is one reason it is critical that we understand the power and allure of the occult.

It's not exclusively a youth problem, however. Large numbers of adults are flocking to the new kinds of spirituality being offered today. When you hear a Hollywood celebrity gushing with excitement about the "revival" of interest in the spiritual world, you can probably hold your applause. Most of it is demonic.

I learned early in my ministry the hold that occultic activities can have on a person. I was speaking to a group of teens one night, and as I finished my message on being wholly committed to Christ, I saw a young man weeping quietly. I asked him if there was anything I could do, but he said no. I continued to talk to him, because I knew something had to be wrong for a teenaged boy to let girls see him crying. Finally he told me he had been deeply involved in the game Dungeons & Dragons®. I offered to pray with him, so we went to a room together to pray.

He told me, "Mr. Logan, I didn't just play Dungeons & Dragons. I was a dungeon master [an expert in the game who memorizes books full of intricate rules]. But last year I destroyed all of my books and got rid of my computer disk. Something still isn't right, though."

He confessed his involvement and asked God to take back the ground he had yielded to Satan through this demonic game that involves the use of power and diabolical planning. As I prayed against the enemy, this young man's chair was thrown backward, his head was thrown back, his eyes rolled back in his head, and he began making gurgling noises. I commanded the enemy to leave in the name and authority of Christ, and everything stopped immediately. The heaviness was gone from his spirit, and he went home free in Christ.

This young man called me not long ago to tell me he is now in seminary, studying to be a pastor. I asked him if he ever had a recurrence of this kind of trouble, and he said no.

I'd like to tell you that every young person who dabbles in occultic games and activities comes to the realization, as this young man did, that these things are bad news. But that wouldn't be true. If it were, a good portion of my counseling appointments could be canceled!

"Harmless" Beginnings

The dangerous thing about occultic activity is that it often begins in such seemingly harmless ways. It begins by dabbling. Most teenagers don't sit around saying, "Let's open our lives up to all kinds of weird experiences and satanic influence so we can have horrible nightmares and compulsive thoughts about suicide." Now, some people do deliberately turn themselves over to Satan, but they're not the majority.

No, it usually starts at a sleepover or party when the kids get bored and someone says, "Hey, want to have some fun? Let's get the Ouija® board. It's really neat. You can ask it real personal questions, and it answers you." Sounds pretty harmless to a teenager, so he or she dabbles. But I also know of cases where adults remember Ouija board predictions made years earlier and live in great fear of their fulfillment.

Whenever I counsel someone who is having demonic problems, one of the first areas I deal with is possible occultic involvement. Most Christians recognize that the occult is real. God's Word specifically forbids contact with evil spirits and those who practice what we would call today occult activities (see Leviticus 19:31). Paul lists witchcraft as one of the "works of the flesh" that believers are to have nothing to do with (Galatians 5:20). But when it comes to the occult, many of God's people do have two major blind spots. One is the extent to which occult practices, even prior to conversion, can affect a believer's walk with Christ.

The second is the extent to which Christians today, particularly young people, are being deceived and led into destructive occult activity by the enemy through things such as music and fantasy games.

We'll consider both of these after we discuss occultism a little more thoroughly.

Reasons for Occult Involvement

There are basically four reasons people go into the occult in some fashion.

Power

Remember the teen who asked me if he would lose his occult powers if he renounced Satan's work in his life? When I replied that he would, Scott rejected his freedom, because he feared he would be "just like everyone else." This is the first reason people are drawn into the occult: power. They want power over their own lives and/or over the lives of other people. College students have told me this is one reason they are attracted to the New Age movement, the promise of control.

I had a man come to my office recently who was an expert in an old practice called "water witching" or "water divining" (the names themselves should tell you something). He was using welding rods to find plastic water pipes underground. That happens to be on our checklist of occult activities, but he got really upset with me.

"I don't see anything wrong with it," he said. "I can find pipes five feet under the ground. I just walk and the rods go down."

It just so happened that my prayer partner that week was an engineering professor. He was sitting there with me while I counseled this man, and said, "That is scientifically impossible. Water isn't magnetic, and neither are plastic pipes."

"It's not scientific, it's demonic," I told the man. "You need to renounce it." He wasn't too excited about that.

Mark Bubeck, the director of our center, grew up on a farm in the Midwest. He tells of a man coming to the farm one day to find water using a divining rod. The rod swished down, and they marked the spot.

Then the man offered to let Mark try it. Mark, who was a teenager then, walked over the same spot with the stick, but nothing happened.

"Walk this way, Mark," the diviner said. Again, nothing happened. Mark tried it once more with no results, when finally the man said, "Here, let me put my hands on your hands." This time, when they walked over the spot, Mark says the stick went down so hard that it almost tore his wrists. The power wasn't in the stick or the water, but in the man. And it was not of God.

Guidance

A second reason for occult involvement is guidance. This is so popular today you can now just call a psychic on a 900 toll line and for a few dollars get your future told. It's one modern-day application of very ancient practices (Deuteronomy 18:9–14).

Many people have played with Ouija boards and have had frightening or eerie experiences. One was a high school student whose parents encouraged him to come and see me. He had begun to exhibit signs of deep depression. When his parents asked him what was wrong, he told them that all he could think about was suicide. For example, when he was driving he would think about driving off a cliff that was on his way to school, hitting another car head-on, or running into the concrete embankment. He could not get these thoughts to stop.

As he entered my office, this young man began to shake violently and sweat profusely. I asked him what was wrong, but he said he didn't know. I asked him when these thoughts of death first started. He said they had started about three months earlier after he and a friend had played with a homemade Ouija board and all the messages to him were the same: he was going to die that year.

He confessed that his seeking of guidance through this Ouija board was a sin, and he asked God to take back the ground he had yielded to Satan. We commanded the enemy to leave and the shaking stopped immediately. In its place he had a deeper inner peace. This was a number of years ago, and he has never had a recurrence of this problem.

Some people look to Ouija boards for guidance. Millions of others direct their lives by what their horoscopes tell them to do. And I doubt if you'll ever find many fortune tellers standing in the unemployment line. Everybody is looking for that little edge, whether in romance or business.

Healing

Healing is a third reason for occult involvement. We hear a lot about this kind of thing occurring overseas, such as the psychic healers in some Asian countries. But people in this country also seek physical help through occult means.

I know of a Christian mother who was told to bring the saliva of her family members on carefully marked slides so a determination could be made of the vitamins and minerals each family member needed.

The woman doing the evaluation asked the mother if she would like to see how it was done. The mother said yes, and went to the back of the store to watch. One of the slides was placed under a pendulum, which immediately swung and pointed to the vitamins that particular family member needed. Needless to say, that mother made a hasty exit for the door.

That process is demonic, no doubt about it. The power that moved the pendulum was not from the scientific but the spirit world. These things take all kinds of forms. I was just told recently about a process whereby a photo of a sick person is put into a machine that reads the person's "aura," the light given off by a person. Based on that reading, a diagnosis is made and the needed medicine is sent to the sick person via radio waves. If the sick person dies, the machine will know because the aura will disappear.

Protection

The fourth and final reason that people are drawn to the occult is protection. Many occult practitioners believe that the spirits can protect them from harm. I've done a lot of ministry among Native Americans and had some eye-opening experiences that I'll share as we go along.

The story of the great Indian warrior Geronimo is a fascinating study of otherworldly power. Geronimo was not a chief but a medicine man. (I can tell you from firsthand experience that medicine men have real powers.) Geronimo believed that his potion made it impossible for him to die from the white soldiers' bullets.

Geronimo would charge head-on into the battle, which freaked out the soldiers fighting him. It was said that Geronimo was shot six times in battle, but he did not die by a bullet. But remember: the issue in occult activities is not that these things work. The issue is, who is making them work?

The Danger of Occult Practices

There is no denying that Satan has power. We can thank God that the enemy's power is limited and that God is firmly in control. But Satan and his forces have power nevertheless, and when someone gives himself over to Satan, his power can be manifested in that person's life.

The Danger of False Spiritualities

A key danger in dabbling in the occult is that another spiritual power will invade one's life. Dr. Samuelson, a friend of mine who is an emergency room physician, prays every day before leaving for the hospital that God will give him wisdom and discernment as he treats his patients. One day, the doctor was getting ready to see a woman who had been brought to emergency because she was totally out of touch with reality. As he walked into the room silently praying for wisdom, the woman suddenly sat up on the gurney, looked straight at him, and said, "Stop praying for me."

That really scared him. How did she know he was praying? She was in such bad shape that he had to commit her to the psychiatric ward of the hospital. Later Dr. Samuelson called me and described the encounter. "Jim, what's her problem?" he asked.

I told him that she was probably involved in occult activities, and to check with the chief psychiatrist for a follow-up report. He did, and the psychiatrist—a nonbeliever—told him she was the worst case he

HIGHER GROUND:
Breaking Occult Bondage

The following action steps can remove occult involvement from your life and return you to higher ground in your relationship with God. Even if you believe you have not surrendered ground to Satan through occult involvement, practice step one, and periodically read the remaining steps to confirm your abstinence from the occult.

1. Make a commitment to God that you will stand against Satan's ways and works in your life, and that you want to be committed to the Lord Jesus Christ.

2. Ask God to reveal any and all occult activity that has taken place in your life:
   a. Renounce the seeking of power as sin and commit yourself to the empowering of God's Holy Spirit.
   b. Renounce the seeking of guidance from evil spirits and commit yourself to guidance from the Scriptures.
   c. Renounce all occult healing involvement and commit yourself to the God who heals (*Jehovah Rapha*) and to God-honoring healing.
   d. Renounce the use of all mantras, charms, medals, or any other object you have trusted in for protection and commit yourself to God's protection (Psalm 91:1–2).

3. Remove all occult material from your home. Burn what can be burned and break and bury what cannot be burned (see Acts 19:19).

4. Ask God to take back all ground given to Satan through your involvement in darkness and wrong music.

5. Commit yourself to listen only to music that is strong in melody and edifies the Lord Jesus Christ.

6. Remove and destroy all music that does not glorify God. (If you are a young person, enlist the guidance of your parents.)

had seen in his ten years as head of the department. The psychiatrist's assessment was that this woman had traveled into another dimension and was trapped there by other beings.

This happened on Wednesday, but by Friday she was fine and they released her. When the psychiatrist asked her what had happened, she told him she was a New Age channeler who had been taken over by the spirit she was channeling. When the spirit left her, she returned to "normal."

Now I know of at least one secular psychiatrist who believes in the reality and power of the spirit world. Actually, many professionals in the field of psychology and psychiatry are convinced there's something out there in "another dimension." Many believe there are beings called spirits, even though these men and women are usually not Christians. But we must recognize the danger in any ongoing encounter with the occult that spirits can gain access to us.

The ground Satan gains in a person's life is not always taken back without a fight. The problem with occult activity is that once you've been involved, you can't just put these things out of your mind. This is why many believers who were heavily into the occult before they became Christians still struggle, even years after conversion, with the memories and associations of their former life.

The Danger of Wrong Music

In one of my ministry prayer letters, I printed the testimony of a young man who was a satanist, a worshiper of Satan, for most of his early years. He was in several different covens as a teenager, attending worship services where they used music to call evil spirits to manifest themselves and empower the worshipers to commit unspeakable evil. Later, he left his coven and began worshiping Satan on his own.

This young man got saved and dedicated his life to the Lord. But certain music still triggers horrible memories and feelings for him. Here's how he describes it:

> I'm asking God to bring healing from my involvement in satanism and the horrors of those early years of my life. Whenever I hear rock music, whether it's supposedly Christian or not, my reaction is extreme. I can't handle it. I don't care what the words say; as soon as I hear the beat, it takes me back to those services where we called the enemy to empower us to do great evil.

I counseled with him and took him through the steps to freedom, and we're trusting God to do a real work in his life. But my point is that even as a Christian who was years removed from his satanic worship days, this man still underwent terrific struggles.

I'm well aware that if you want to get a lively argument started, all you have to do is bring up the subject of music styles and preferences. Books have been written on the subject, and I doubt that Christians will ever come to complete agreement on what's proper or acceptable in music. My purpose is not to write a treatise on music. All I know is that when the enemy wants to control and eventually destroy a person, music is often his weapon of choice. Someone has said that if he could control the music of a nation, he could control that nation.

I agree. I could fill the rest of this book with the testimonies of teenagers and young adults who were driven to destructive, murderous, and suicidal thoughts by the music they listened to as part of their ever-deepening occult activity. One missionary kid said,

> Regardless of what anyone says, these songs stay with a person for the rest of their lives. I haven't listened to '666' in over 5 years, or even seen the record, yet I can still sing half of the songs if I want to. It's a great trick Satan uses to get my mind off God.

Another teenager sat in my office recently under the oppressive influence of evil spirits. We just could not seem to break the enemy's influence over his life.

Finally I said, "Let's pray together and ask God's Holy Spirit to bring to your mind just what it is that's hindering your freedom."

As we finished praying, he said, "Music—I listen to the wrong music, and that's why I'm not free."

"Would you be willing to confess this to God?" I asked. "Would you be willing to place your music on God's altar and under the guidance of God and your parents, destroy all your wrong music when you go home?"

When this young man gave his music to God in prayer and told God he would destroy it as God and his parents led him, he was set free.

We know that spirits respond to music. David drove the evil spirit from Saul by playing for him (1 Samuel 16:23). Over the years I've seen the unbelievable power music has to influence people's lives. And it's not just in this country or the Western world. The use of music in occult spirit worship is worldwide, and the music used is all very similar in its beat.

There's a lot more I could say, but it's safe to draw this conclusion: Music is one of the tools the enemy uses to entice people into the occult, and the effects often stay with these people long after their conversion to Christ.

The Danger of Fantasy

We've already seen that fantasy games are another open door into the occult—and many are the Christian young people who have entered therein! A few years ago games like Dungeons & Dragons were very popular with kids. Today Dungeons & Dragons and other occult simulation games are available on floppy and CD-ROM computer disks. In the more sophisticated CD versions, viewers receive the colors, depth, resolution (from digitized images), and full-motion video action that draw young viewers deeply into the game, leaving strong images that approach reality.

I was speaking to a group of young people one time and was warning them about the game when a thirteen-year-old challenged me. "I don't see anything wrong with it. I play it well, and it's my favorite game. You shouldn't be saying those things."

I said, "Any game that requires you to rape, kill, put curses on people, and quote from the satanic bible isn't fit for you to be playing."

I'm not saying that every time a person listens to a rock song or plays a fantasy game he will be fighting demons. What I am saying is that all of these things open the door to Satan's influence and give him a tremendous amount of ground on which to build his strongholds.

What many Christian young people consider to be harmless music or games can be powerful tools in the hands of the enemy. And I'm afraid we haven't seen anything yet. The "virtual reality" craze that has landed with full force upon us gives the enemy a wide new avenue down which to parade his temptations. Through advances in computer technology, adults—and children—can don headwear that encloses their field of vision to view action on a miniature TV screen that gives a heightened sense of reality through the use of color and three dimensional images. Though this could have positive implications for learning (business and medical schools can use this for training professionals) and includes clean entertainment (learning how to swing a golf club, for instance), it has just begun being exploited for pornographic and occult experiences.

With virtual reality, for example, a man by turning his head or touching a keypad can make a three dimensional woman in his field of view respond accordingly. This is not simply seeing an object but participating in an experience. The viewer becomes part of the scene, which responds to his actions. Thus he can have a prostitute in his imagination without going to a house of prostitution; similarly, a woman viewer can "participate" in an occult activity without leaving her home, as a CD-ROM spins out various scenarios before her eyes according to her selected choices. Technology experts predict that eventually computers will respond according to changes in your pulse rate, perspiration, or breathing pattern.

"It goes to your psyche," a friend told me after trying one of the interactive games, using just a keyboard and a computer screen. He returned that game and several others that he refused to open. "It involves you totally. It's really creepy." What seems to be harmless entertainment can draw you into new experiences that leave you open to satanic influence.

The Danger of Occult Objects

Before we consider how to break occult bondage, let's consider a very different way a person can give ground to the enemy in these areas and not even be aware of it: association with occultic objects. Leonard had been a missionary in Taiwan for two years when he had what appeared to be a nervous breakdown. He suffered from debilitating fear, insomnia, depression, and a restless spirit.

Despite seeing fifteen different counselors and psychologists and finally winding up in a missionary recovery center, his problems persisted. According to his letter to me, it wasn't until years later that he began to feel the root of his problem might be the two years he spent traveling from one idolatrous temple to another taking pictures.

"I wanted to see firsthand the ways and works of the enemy," Leonard wrote. "This was a very foolish thing to do, as I unknowingly opened myself up to demonic attack. I assumed that as a tourist, I would be unharmed. The Lord has used the book, *The Adversary,* by Mark Bubeck, to confirm my suspicions. All of my symptoms were listed as having possible demonic origin."

Once he realized what was happening, this missionary and his brother prayed and asked God to set him free. Leonard was liberated instantly and began his long road to recovery.

The Danger of Curiosity

In this case curiosity almost killed the missionary, let alone the cat. We are not to be curious about the things of evil. King David said he would not even take the names of false gods on his lips (Psalm 16:4).

God told Israel to burn the images of false gods and not take any of the things from pagan lands into their houses, lest they become a curse (Deuteronomy 7:25–26). It's a very dangerous thing to be an observer of occult things or participate in any way in occult practices. But if you go as a rescuer, like missionary Amy Carmichael who went into pagan temples in India to rescue young girls from temple prostitution, you'll have God's protection.

That's why I always strongly warn Christians to be careful of what they do and where they go, and what they bring into their homes. I got a call from a Christian family whose teenaged son was a big fan of Stephen King, the number one writer of horror books today. This boy had a lot of King's books in the house, some of them his own and some from the library.

The parents weren't aware of the contents of the books until their son began having terror attacks. They burned the books he owned, hoping this would stop the attacks. But when they did that, strange things began happening around the house—much as they might happen in a Stephen King novel or movie! Appliances would turn off and on by themselves. They heard knocking on doors when no one was there, and things moved by themselves.

Needless to say, the family was being terrorized by these frightening things. Who wouldn't be? The boy's curiosity about evil and the occult had opened him to demonic influence. I counseled this young man that as a Christian, he needed to renounce his involvement in the occult by reading such sinister stories. He did so, and I haven't heard any report of problems since. But his curiosity about things evil, powerful, and otherworldly had let him yield ground to demonic influence.

The Danger of Family Involvement

We'll talk more in a later chapter about the issue of ancestral spirits and the passing on of the iniquities of the father "unto the third and fourth generation" (Numbers 14:18). This phenomenon is especially powerful when it comes to the occult.

I've seen this in my work with Sioux and Apache Indians, where a medicine man would discern which one of his children the spirits had selected to inherit his powers. Everyone in the tribe knew who had these powers.

I have even heard reports of occult powers in my own family. Once I called one of my aunts and was surprised when her daughter, my cousin, answered the phone. I hadn't seen her in decades and she had been living in Utah, her mother in California.

When I asked her what she was doing in town, she said her mother, my aunt, was very sick and had called her in Mexico, where she was on a hunting trip, to come home. She had arrived just in time to get her mother to the hospital and save her life. Otherwise, she would have died from a bowel obstruction.

"That's really something," I said. "How in the world did your mother find you in Mexico?"

I'll never forget her answer. "Jim," she said, "she didn't call me on the phone. She called me in her mind." They had used mental telepathy, and often talked this way.

Then I remembered that this aunt used to tell fortunes—accurately. I used to watch her do this when I was a teenager. I tried to get her to do it for me, but she said she could only do it when the "special feeling" came on her. My mother later told me this aunt got her training in fortune-telling from her mother, my grandmother.

Since I found all of this out, I have done some heavy-duty praying at the Logan house. I don't want any of this power to pass on to my grandchildren, all of whom have received Christ.

Renouncing the Hidden Things of Darkness

It should be obvious by now that anyone who enters the world of the occult is on Satan's territory, his ground. If we give ground to Satan when we sin, imagine the hold he has on those who give themselves to occult practices at whatever level.

1. Renounce Satan's Hold

The steps to freedom for people trapped in the occult are similar to those we use to help those with other problems. When people come to me for help who have been involved in the occult to whatever degree, the first thing I have them do is renounce Satan's hold on their lives. It has to start here if they want to be free.

I point them to that wonderful passage in Revelation 12, where the people of God overcame Satan by "the blood of the Lamb, and by the word of their testimony; and they loved not their lives unto the death" (v. 11). What a marvelous picture. These people testified that they would rather die than compromise with the forces of evil.

2. Declare Your Intent

It's vital that the person renounces the enemy's work in his or her life. Otherwise, how can we help someone who isn't sure he wants to take back the ground he has given to Satan? If you are involved in activities, with objects, or people that are demonic, you need to declare aloud to Satan your intent to serve Jesus. I ask my counselees to make this declaration of intent: "Satan, I don't want anything more to do with your ways or works in my life. I want to be totally committed to the Lord Jesus Christ."

For many people with occult problems, this may be the first time they have ever stood against evil. My experience is that when a person does this, he can come under tremendous attack. It's as if Satan says, "So you want to fight, eh?" When people sincerely repent and renounce the work of Satan in their lives, they initally feel better, but many areas may still need to be dealt with.

By the way, people trapped in occultism aren't the only ones who need to renounce Satan's influence. All of us as believers are called to say no to Satan each day and be obedient to Christ. I'm not talking about anything extreme, just a daily commitment not to yield to the enemy's ways or works but to be faithful to the Lord.

Three Important Reminders

Let me make three observations in closing this chapter. First, when a person makes a clean break with the occult, he or she usually has some occult paraphernalia that should be gotten rid of. If you have such items, destroy these occult materials yourself. I never do it for anyone. My philosophy is, "You bought it, you burn it."

Second, remember that God never tells us to put away something and then just leave ourselves empty (Matthew 12:43–45). Whenever we remove something, we are to replace it with something. People trapped in the occult need to have that evil influence replaced by the truth of God's Word.

Third, anyone who has ever had deep occult involvement will tell you: getting into the occult is relatively easy. Getting out, in contrast, is very traumatic. But it is essential for spiritual health. The result will be freedom and wholeness. None of God's people has any business dabbling in this dangerous world. Instead, we can renounce it and find inner peace as a result of obedience to God's Word.

—4—
LOOKING BACKWARD: UNFORGIVENESS AND BITTERNESS

I am unaware of any survey being conducted to measure the number of Bible-believing Christians who have had experiences with the occult. If someone were to take such a survey in the average evangelical church, I suspect the percentage of people for whom the occult is a major problem would be small. At least, I hope it would.

I'm not downplaying by any means the tremendous power the occult can have in a person's life. But if Ouija boards and fortune-tellers have never been a problem for you, Satan probably won't tempt you heavily in that area. He's much too smart for that. He doesn't waste any of his "fiery darts."

His tactic may be like that of any effective warrior. I remember a conversation I had with several Sioux Indians during my work among them. We were talking about those old Western movies where the Indians are firing huge volleys of arrows at the wagon trains. "Is that the way Sioux warriors did it?" I asked.

Their answer was fascinating. "Are you kidding? Have you ever made an arrow by hand? Every time a Sioux warrior let an arrow fly, he expected to hear an ouch. Every arrow counted."

That's a great picture of the way Satan works. He doesn't just fling his arrows of temptation around. He expects every arrow to hit the mark.

So if the occult world is a foreign place to you, I say great. Praise the Lord. It holds no allure for me either. But the enemy knows where each of us is vulnerable, and that's the spot he aims for.

In this and the next few chapters we are going to deal with areas that are major problems for many believers; areas in which God's people, including parents and their children, are giving tremendous ground to the enemy to attack them. The first of these is the area of bitterness and unforgiveness.

A Story of Forgiveness

If I had to sum up the message of the Scriptures in one word, it would be the word *forgiveness*. The Bible is the story of how God forgives. It begins in Genesis and continues through Revelation. Along the way we see God reaching out to people to forgive them.

Now if forgiveness is one of the central themes of Bible—perhaps the central theme—where do you suppose the enemy might attack you and me as God's children? Through unforgiveness. How can I go and tell other men and women the good news that they can be forgiven by God when I am harboring unforgiveness in my own heart? In fact, when unforgiveness and bitterness rule my heart, I'm moving backward in my relationships with people and God, and I'm opening myself up to Satan's attacks.

Forgiving Others

How did Jesus Himself teach us to pray? One of His requests in His model prayer was "Forgive us our debts, as we forgive our debtors" (Matthew 6:12). That's a heavy-duty request, isn't it? Jesus isn't talking about forgiveness in regard to salvation here, but the kind of forgiveness we are to extend to others precisely because we are forgiven people. This is forgiveness that keeps us in proper fellowship with Him.

Hebrews 12:15 speaks powerfully to the dangers of allowing a "root of bitterness" to grow in our hearts. The picture of a plant growing from its root is a perfect illustration of what the writer is saying. If the root is bitter, what can the plant produce but bitterness? You can't plant an apple tree and expect figs. Notice how wide-ranging the effects of bitterness are. "Many" will be defiled if bitterness is allowed to grow in the hearts of God's people.

But Christians don't like to admit they're bitter. What do Christians say? "I've been hurt," or "I have resentments." I'm not denying the fact that we can be hurt by others. But resentments are bitterness in the crib, just waiting to grow up into full-fledged bitterness. We need to call it by its worst name and see it for what it is.

Getting It All Out

I have a silk dandelion in a flowerpot on my desk. It's a great teaching tool. When I ask people what kind of flower it is, they usually say, "That's not a flower. It's a dandelion, a weed."

"You're right," I reply. "It is a weed. If I wanted to get rid of dandelions, how would I do it? By pulling off the petals and throwing them away?"

"No."

"Could I just mow over them with the lawn mower? Would that take care of my problem?"

"No."

"Right again. There's only one way to get rid of a dandelion. Pull it up, roots and all."

Most readily agree. And that's what we must do to clear bitterness from our lives. We must recognize it is a weed—a sin—and pull it all out. Suppose your doctor gives you the bad news that you have cancer and need surgery. You have the operation, and as you're coming out of the anesthetic the doctor walks into your room. What's the first thing you want to know? "Did you get it all?"

"We got most of it." Is that very comforting? It's the same with bitterness and resentments. If we don't get it, roots and all, it will grow up and many will be affected and defiled by it. It's not just a secret thing when I harbor wrong feelings in my heart.

Suffering and Bitterness

The apostle Peter in his first epistle teaches us much about bitterness that can come from suffering. First Peter is a treatise on how to respond to suffering. Clearly Peter has no room for the false gospel of the 1990s that if you become a Christian, everything is going to be wonderful.

That preaching is false. Christians and non-Christians go through the same life experiences—with one big difference. God's people don't have to go through their suffering alone. When Jesus died on the cross, the darkness surrounded Him and He cried out in agony. Jesus went through His darkness all alone so that I don't have to go through my darkness alone.

But we all suffer. In fact, 1 Peter 4:19 says suffering is God's will for His people. This is a verse you won't see hanging on too many decorative wall plaques. But I'll say this. If our Christianity doesn't work in suffering, we don't have much to offer anyone.

All of this is relevant to the issue of bitterness and unforgiveness because these feelings are usually triggered when we are called to suffer, especially when we have been wrongfully treated by others. In fact, Peter concludes chapter 4 with a discussion of how to respond to suffering that comes when someone treats you unfairly for your devotion to Christ. (See 4:14–19; note also 2:19–24.)

Getting Rid of Bitterness

Removing bitterness from our lives requires three steps. Each one is vital; a person must take all three steps or the process won't work. Remember, Satan will not let go easily of any ground I have yielded to him through bitterness or some other sin.

For an example of how to respond to suffering and avoid bitterness, we are to look at Jesus, according to Peter.

> This is thankworthy, if a man for conscience toward God endure grief, suffering wrongfully. For what glory is it, if, when ye be buffeted for your faults, ye shall take it patiently? but if, when ye do well, and suffer for it, ye take it patiently, this is acceptable with God. For even hereunto were ye called: because Christ also suffered for us, leaving us an example, that we should follow in his steps: who did no sin, neither was guile found in his mouth: who, when he was reviled, reviled not again; when he suffered, he threatened not; but committed himself to him that judgeth righteously. (1 Peter 2:19–23)

Jesus is our example here. Sometimes we suffer unjustly. Other times we reap the consequences of bad decisions. Our words and actions are improper; we say things we ought not say, and we do things we ought not do. But Jesus never said or did anything wrong. His suffering was wholly unjust. But rather than retaliating or becoming bitter when He suffered, He "committed himself to him that judgeth righteously." Jesus knew that His Father would always do what was right. So He was able to say to God, "I commit this to You because I know You will do what is right." Here is the first step in ridding ourselves of bitterness. (See "Higher Ground" (page 64) for specific ways to put the following three steps into practice.)

1. Identify and Release

Step one in getting rid of bitterness is to identify those who have hurt you and be willing to release them to God so He can deal with them (Romans 12:19). Peter says that when we do wrong and bear the suffering for it, there's no praise in that. But if a person whose conscience is clear before God suffers for something he didn't do and commits it to the Lord, He can be honored through it.

I saw a marvelous example of this truth demonstrated by a major league baseball player God sent into my life to disciple some years ago. I was able to disciple him at the same time he was discipling other members of his American League team.

Arnie (not his real name) was a utility infielder, an outstanding Christian with a wonderful testimony for Christ. His bubble-gum cards included Romans 10:9–10 with his signature, as did his picture in the team program. Anytime he was interviewed, he always talked about the Lord Jesus.

About this time, the team hired a new manager who was virulently anti-Christian; he despised Arnie's faith and therefore despised Arnie. When this young player was named Christian Athlete of the Year, the manager refused to let him receive his award on the field. "He'll get it in the tunnel under the stands," the manager said—and that's exactly where he got it. Arnie was really mistreated by this manager and was hurting, because he loved baseball.

Not too long after this incident the manager finally sent Arnie down to the minor leagues, not because of his inability to play baseball, but because of his Christian testimony. Arnie reported to the minor league team, but he didn't go down bitter. In fact, he called me one day and told me he knew why he had been sent to the minors—to lead two guys to Christ! Do you suppose if this ballplayer had gone to the minors seething with bitterness God could have used him to lead those players to Christ?

Eventually this outstanding young man came back to the major league team, but the manager insisted that the team either release this player or he would quit. So the team bought out Arnie's contract and he was released. Would you be bitter if you were not allowed to do the one thing you loved most simply because you were a Christian? My ballplayer friend wasn't.

We talked about the situation. The sports reporters were asking him about it, wanting him to tell all. He told me, "I really want to respond to this properly." So he asked to meet with the owner of the team to thank him for the opportunity to be part of a great organization, and so he could leave the team with a clear conscience. Arnie went to the owner's office and expressed his thanks, then turned to leave. But the owner stopped him.

"We can't let a man like you go. I'll give you a job in the organization." And they kept him in the organization. You see, this ballplayer didn't do anything wrong. But he drew from God's grace and reflected Christ in a time of suffering, and his actions brought about God's response.

This first step is so important, because we'll see a little later that Jesus Himself said bitterness gives ground to the enemy. Learning how to deal with bitterness is also vital because suffering isn't an option for us. It's our calling as Christians to suffer (1 Peter 2:21a).

But if you can't trust God when things are bad, you open yourself up to bitterness. Dealing with those who have hurt or wronged you is God's job, not yours (Romans 12:19). When you try to take that respon-

HIGHER GROUND:
Removing Bitterness

If you have not forgiven someone, it's likely you harbor an unforgiving spirit *and bitterness*, for as time passes the resentment over an offense deepens into bitterness. You must forgive. Here's how.

1. Ask God to reveal to your mind the people against whom you are holding feelings that are not right. Make a list of the name(s) as God reveals them. Also, check yourself to see if you are holding any bitterness toward God or yourself, and include these names on your list if that is the case.

2. Start at the bottom of the list, because these are usually the people who are easier to forgive. As you work your way up the list, tell God you forgive each person and release the hurts to Him. That's forgiving from your heart. We are bitter for a reason, and we must get in touch with pain—that is, the reasons we are bitter.

3. If after forgiving the person for the major offense you recall a specific, hurtful incident, don't let your feelings smolder anew. Instead, release them to God then and there. In my experience with my own father I found that after dealing with the major offenses, I would remember days or weeks later a specific incident. I would stop and pray, "God, I forgive my dad for _____ (the specific offense) also." You only need to deal with the things God brings to your remembrance.

4. Tell God you are willing to live with the ongoing consequences of the offender's action and share these with Him in prayer.

5. Ask God to take back the ground you have given Satan through unforgiveness, then turn around and reach for the things that are ahead.

6. If some future action of a person you have forgiven triggers painful memories and you are tempted to pick up past bitterness, release this temptation to God on the spot.

sibility upon yourself, you free God of any responsibility to act on your behalf.

We've already seen that suffering is a given. It's coming, so it's much better to be prepared for it ahead of time and know how to respond. As Peter wrote,

> Forasmuch then as Christ hath suffered for us in the flesh, arm yourselves likewise with the same mind: for he that hath suffered in the flesh hath ceased from sin; that he no longer should live the rest of his time in the flesh to the lusts of men, but to the will of God. (1 Peter 4:1–2)

How do we arm ourselves with the same mind as Christ in suffering? By not retaliating but committing it to God. This is a real struggle for many of the people who come to our counseling center. The issue is, can we really trust God when we suffer? I can tell you, this was a terrible struggle for me. I've mentioned the unhappiness of my home life and the awful feelings I had growing up.

Those wounds affected me well into my adulthood, and I had tremendous bitterness against God for the suffering I endured at the hands of my father. Then I went to an Institute in Basic Youth Conflicts seminar in 1968 where the speaker, Bill Gothard, told me that God had placed me in my family.

That really stunned me. I thought to myself, I can't believe this guy is saying this stuff. He's off the wall. God wouldn't put me in a home where I was verbally abused and put down all my life, would He?

Bill was right, of course. God in His wisdom gives us the right family setting in which He can work. No family background is too difficult for God to work through. Many of the people I counsel with are bitter toward God for the things that have happened to them, even being placed in a particular family. But it's hard for them to admit their bitterness, just as it was hard for me years earlier to realize I was actually bitter toward God for my family life.

Bitterness is making God accountable to me. It's also an affront to His sovereignty. In effect, we're saying, "God, I don't like what You're doing, and I want You to know it. You didn't ask my permission or check with me ahead of time, and I'm angry."

In the last part of verse 1, Peter also says that suffering is part of God's purifying process to help us get rid of sin. Sometimes we pray "Lord, I want to be godly," then we shove away all the tools by which He wants to purify us. Often when a tough time comes, the first thing we say is, "Why me?" (see v. 12).

God's answer is, "Why not you?" It's a good question. Why should you or I be excluded from the "fiery trial"? We want to be godly, but often we don't want the refining fires. When they hit, we become resentful and bitter in the process of becoming godly. Isn't that amazing? We become bitter because God didn't do it the way we expected.

When I think of fiery trials, I think of the prophet Daniel's three friends (Daniel 3). When they were thrown into the furnace, what burned? Just the ropes that bound them. That's all. God wants to burn the ropes that have us in bondage.

And as Peter wrote in verse 13, rather than turn bitter in trials, we are to rejoice. Why? Because the glory of God rests upon us.

Corrie ten Boom recounted a tale of great suffering in her epic of faith to God, *The Hiding Place.* Her Dutch father died for hiding Jews from the Nazis, and Corrie and her sister Betsie endured great pain in the Ravensbruck concentration camp, with Betsie eventually dying at the camp. Years before Corrie wrote *The Hiding Place,* I heard her speak. Here was this little Dutch lady who suffered so terribly for serving God, but who chose to trust Him and forgive rather than turn bitter: in a moving climax to the book, she forgave the guard who had mistreated her and Betsie. Millions of lives were touched because of her obedience. As I listened to her speak that night, the glow of God was on that woman's face.

2. Forgive from the Heart

Step two in getting rid of bitterness is found in Matthew 18:21–22: "Then came Peter to him, and said, 'Lord, how oft shall my brother sin against me, and I forgive him? till seven times?' Jesus saith unto him, 'I say not unto thee, Until seven times, but, Until seventy times seven.'" If I am going to be free of bitterness, I must be willing to forgive people from the heart. When Peter asked at what point he could stop forgiving someone, Jesus answered by calling for unlimited forgiveness.

Every time a person hurts me, I must forgive. Most of us have heard Jesus' words so often we miss the significance of what He's saying. Imagine what unlimited forgiveness means, for example, to a wife who has an abusive husband. Is there a point at which she can stop forgiving him? She may have to separate herself from him for her own protection, but she still can—and should—forgive him.

Remember Mary in chapter 1? Look at her testimony again (pages 21–22), and you'll notice that in the final paragraph she thanked the Lord for enabling her to avoid the crippling effects of bitterness in her own life while she struggled with her husband's verbal abuse. God empowered Mary to put away bitterness and resentment toward her husband. Instead, she began to return his rejection with Christlike love.

The only thing that made this testimony possible was a wife who decided to trust God for the grace to forgive her husband and let Him take care of the results.

Notice that after Jesus' call for endless forgiveness in Matthew 18, He told a story (v. 23–34) about forgiveness. The numbers in the story are staggering: this servant owed the king $10 million, but was forgiven. A second servant owed the first servant a few dollars in comparison, but the forgiven servant refused to forgive him. As a result, he was turned over to "the tormentors" by the king (v. 34). Jesus didn't want us to miss the application of this amazing story of unforgiveness, so He gave it to us Himself (v. 35). If we hold resentments and unforgiveness in our hearts against anyone, the same thing will happen to us. We will give the enemy ground to torment us.

We also find this same idea in the church age. In 1 Corinthians 5:1–5, Paul writes about a sin in the church that was so bad it was offensive even to the local unbelievers. What was this man's judgment? To be delivered to Satan (v. 5).

In the New Testament, church discipline was turning the offender over to demonic forces (see also 1 Timothy 1:20). The spiritual protection of the church was removed from this person and the enemy was free to wreak havoc on him—even "for the destruction of the flesh."

But the man at Corinth repented, and the church didn't know what to do (2 Corinthians 2:1–11). "Forgive him," Paul says (v. 7), and then adds his own forgiveness (v. 10). Do this, he says, "Lest Satan should get an advantage of us: for we are not ignorant of his devices" (v. 11). Bitterness and a refusal to forgive others are Satan's devices that open a person to demonic attacks and damage the body of Christ, and Paul knew that.

As I said in an earlier chapter, the problem today is that we are ignorant of Satan's works and ways. For instance, researchers report that the divorce rate among believers is as bad as it is among unbelievers. Unforgiving spouses infect and tear down many marriages.

How much unforgiveness do you suppose is involved in divorce? If you don't know how to forgive, don't get married. Whether you are married or single, remember Jesus commands you to forgive. And we are not to forgive artificially or halfheartedly. We must forgive others fully, from our hearts. That is, we must get in touch with the pain of the offense and release it to God by forgiving the person by name for the specific offenses that caused the pain. "God, I forgive _____ (the offender) for _____ (the offense)."

3. Live with the Consequences

The third and final step in releasing bitterness is a willingness to live with the ongoing consequences of the offender's actions. This is the most difficult step of all if it applies. Yet it is essential if we are to escape the consequences of a bitter spirit and honor God by obeying

Him. The key to being willing to live with the consequences is to maintain vital contact with the Holy Spirit. Ephesians 4:30–32 says this is essential if we want to be successful in spiritual warfare. We're told not to grieve the Holy Spirit, and then in the very next phrase we are told, "Let all bitterness . . . be put away from you" (v. 31). Anger is mentioned too. Many bitter people also struggle with anger.

Notice what we are to replace all of the sinful acts in verse 31 with: forgiveness. And not just any forgiveness. We are to forgive the way Jesus forgave us—completely. He forgave us an eternal debt. All we are asked to do is forgive temporal debts.

A man I'll call Jack remains the finest example I've seen of someone willing to forgive and live with the consequences of another person's actions. Jack called my office tired of his deep depression. "I've been everywhere for help. Can I come and see you?" he asked. I was very skeptical about what I could do, because I knew the counselors he had seen were good people. But he insisted, so I gave him an appointment for a future date.

Just before he was to come, his wife called me and asked if she could come too. "I know why he's depressed, but he doesn't know," she said.

Do you ever get curious? Her statement made me curious—although this was one time I wished I hadn't been. So I asked her what she meant.

"My husband has a low sperm count," she began. "We know that God opens and closes the womb, and we wanted a large family, so we committed ourselves to God for children. We've had several children since that time and my husband is so excited. But what he doesn't know is that these aren't his children. They were fathered by someone else." This breach in the marriage covenant was putting this man under great spiritual oppression.

I won't share any more of the sordid details. I almost got sick when I heard that. This was the weekend, and this couple was due to come on Monday. I didn't want to see them. I was praying for Christ's return, anything to avoid having to face this.

I thought of my four children. What a horrible thing for a father to have to discover, and it was going to be in my office. I know what bitterness can do to people, and I wondered if this man would exercise God's grace to accept and deal with this. When I sat down with Jack and his wife, I took them through the three steps we have just outlined. Let me briefly explain how I do that with every counselee, and then this couple's response.

The first thing I do is go through what the Scriptures say about bitterness so the counselee can see it in the Bible. I never ask anyone to make a commitment to something until he has seen it in Scripture. The only thing that sets people free is the truth and their commitment to it. I ask, "Are you willing to commit to this? Are you willing to line your life up with the truth?"

If the person is willing, I ask him to pray that God will reveal to him the people he has not forgiven from his heart. People must deal with the pain and hurt before they are truly free. Are people usually bitter for no reason? No, something has happened. So when someone says, "I forgive so-and-so," I ask, "What do you forgive them for?" The counselee must face that.

Then I write down the names on a legal pad and we pray through the list again: family, friends, former friends, people at church, work, or school, whoever has hurt this person. I read the names and the counselee tells God he forgives that person and what they did to him.

You can take these steps in your own life. Get alone with God and ask Him to reveal to you people toward whom you are harboring bad feelings. You don't need someone else there unless you can't be objective. Make a list of the names, the things that happened, and any ongoing consequences. Pray through that list and forgive the people on it— including God and yourself if necessary.

Well, God did an amazing work of grace in the hearts of this man and his wife. She confessed her sin and made it right with everyone involved, asking God's forgiveness and the forgiveness of her husband for what she had done to him and their family.

Jack seemingly had the greater amount of forgiveness to bestow. When she admitted her sin, Jack could easily have felt the sting and anger of betrayal. Not only had his wife broken their marriage vows through her adultery, but she had borne children by another man that Jack would have to love as his own. Yet Jack, who loved his wife and his God, found it relatively easy to forgive his wife and the other fellow. The hard part was facing the consequences of that sin every day sitting around his table. I'm glad to report that Jack loves those kids, although he knew some days it would be hard.

Choosing to Forgive

Forgiveness is a choice, not a feeling. When I considered forgiving my own father, I struggled with making that choice, because I didn't feel forgiving toward him. I forgave him as an act of the will. That's why I say obedience precedes understanding.

Years ago, as a a pastor in Tacoma, Washington, I preached an Easter message on forgiveness and the cross. I told how I hated my father but how God taught me to forgive him. On the way home, my wife turned to me and said, "I enjoyed your message this morning. I know you've forgiven your dad, but I don't think you ever asked his forgiveness. Why don't you call him today and ask his forgiveness."

"No, I don't think that's how I want to do it. I want him to see my face when I ask his forgiveness. I can't do that on the phone."

Twenty minutes later, I got a call from my dad, who never called. I told him how bad I felt for my rebelliousness and asked him to forgive me. "Aw, kids will be kids," he said. Right then I knew how much I had hurt him. I asked him again for his forgiveness. He said he forgave me.

The thing I wanted most in my life was my dad's approval, but he had never said one positive thing about me. But after I made the first step, he sent me a letter saying he was proud of me.

In August of that year Dad said he wanted to come alone to visit us, something else he would normally never do. As I watched him walk down the airport concourse toward me, I realized that I loved my father. It was amazing. Love for him just welled up within me. I didn't think it was possible to feel love for my father, because I had hated him so much for so long.

Dad died that Christmas. At the funeral I told all four of his sisters that I asked his forgiveness before he died. Each one of my aunts told me the same thing: "Your dad came back from that time with you and said it was the best week of his life."

Here I was a Christian and a pastor, and my father went into eternity having had only one good week with his son because I held bitterness. Thank God I settled it before he went to the grave. Today I can say that God didn't do a great work in my heart until I dealt with my hatred for my father.

When it comes to forgiving someone who has offended us, we must act in obedience, even when the feelings aren't there. Ephesians 4:32 makes it clear that God is not asking me to feel something, but to do something. When God told Moses to stretch out his staff over the Red Sea, he could have doubted, even being resentful that God had put him in this predicament—the approaching Egyptian army pinning him against the sea and his people, unarmed, tired from the journey, some of them complaining. Moses could have complained and refused.

Instead, he did as God commanded, because it was God who asked and because Moses knew who God is. Faith demands a warrant, a grounds for belief. A warrant is a legal document on which an action is based. God's Word, His promise to act, was the warrant for Moses' faith. We know he had faith because of his actions. That's the way it is with forgiveness. We can respond with forgiveness even when our feelings say no, for God's Word commands us and promises His blessings to those who do forgive.

— 5 —
IT'S ALWAYS RIGHT TO GET RIGHT

According to 1 Timothy 1:19, there are two things you must have to keep from being shipwrecked in the Christian life: faith and a good conscience.

Originally, the apostle Paul made the request of Timothy, so that this young follower might "war a good warfare" (v. 18). If we look briefly at the setting for these words, we can understand why a clear conscience is so important in our spiritual lives. Paul told Timothy to be on his spiritual guard. Why? Because Timothy was serving the Lord in a hotbed of pagan religion and demon activity, the great city of Ephesus. Even the church at Ephesus was being infiltrated by false teachings.

If Timothy was going to fight a good spiritual war, he needed first to hold on to "faith," which in this setting probably refers to the faith, the truth of the gospel, as opposed to false teachings like those Paul refers to earlier in the chapter.

The Importance of a Clear Conscience

Timothy also needed a good conscience to fight a good spiritual war. The spiritual battle at the end of the twentieth century remains the same: along with faith we need a good conscience to encounter temptation. The word *conscience* takes in a lot of territory in the New Testament, but I want to focus on one aspect that I believe is critical to victory over the enemy: the need to keep our conscience clear. Paul himself said he worked hard to keep his conscience clear of any offense toward God and toward others (Acts 24:16).

How important is a good conscience? Paul listed it in 1 Timothy 1:5 as one essential for effective ministry. That, plus the discipline inflicted on Hymenaeus and Alexander for jettisoning their consciences along with their faith (v. 20), suggests that it's extremely important.

Paul is saying, in effect, that one of the several errors these men were propagating was that it's not important for believers to maintain a clear conscience. For this they were turned over to demons in a step of drastic church discipline designed to bring about their repentance.

Remember, these men were believers. You don't have to turn unbelievers over to Satan. They're already his. I can't see any believer saying that faith isn't important. But I can see believers saying that clearing your conscience isn't important, because it's a very difficult thing to do.

The Other Side of the Coin

Why is that? First, though we may be willing to forgive a person who hurts us if he or she comes to us asking our forgiveness and seeking to make things right, many times that never happens. The other person inflicts a wound on us and never does anything about it. Second, we may hurt someone else and never deal with it ourselves. Maintaining a clear conscience demands that we give attention to each of these situations. This is the other side of the coin of bitterness and unforgiveness, discussed in the previous chapter.

Yes, though the offense is against us, and the offender does not confess the wrong or ask forgiveness, we may forgive the person—and perhaps ask the person for forgiveness as well if we have created hurt in our response. In forgiving my dad and asking him to forgive me, even though Dad had not asked me to forgive him (see pages 69–70), I received a clear conscience, as did he, calling our subsequent time together "the best week of my life."

Setting Others Free

That is the other wonderful thing that happens when we clear our conscience. When we seek forgiveness for the hurt we have caused others, we free *them* up from the bitterness they are holding toward us. By allowing others the opportunity to release their bitterness, we may even be helping to remove an excuse from their lives for the enemy to torment them.

That's why I ask my counselees to make a list of the people who have something against them. Until they have done this, they don't really have a clear conscience. I'm not talking about endless introspection or airing all their dirty laundry in public. That's not the idea at all. There are things in all of our lives that need to be kept among the people involved. What happened is not everyone else's business.

The guideline I use is that the scope of the forgiveness need be no greater than the scope of the offense. If we share things about ourselves with people who are not part of the problem or the solution, we may live to regret it.

How to Clear Up Old Offenses

So I'm very careful here, because the people who come to my office are often carrying extremely heavy baggage from the past. It's like a time bomb hidden in a suitcase on an airplane. If that thing goes off, it's going to hurt an awful lot of innocent people. We're only dealing here with people with whom we haven't made things right.

Even in these cases, though, there are times when it's the better part of wisdom to leave some things unsaid. In other words, we don't have a right to spill out all of our confessions if it's going to wreak needless pain and havoc in someone else's life. I tell the people I'm counseling, "If there are people from your past you need to forgive, God is big enough to bring them back into your life."

For example, Bradley wanted to clear his conscience before the Lord concerning two incidents of illicit sex in his past. He wanted to meet the two women and seek their forgiveness, so he prayed that God would give him the opportunity to make things right.

Bradley knew nothing of the two women's lives at the moment. Bradley himself was now married and had gotten his life straight with the Lord. His wife knew he had an immoral past, but she didn't know the details. The past really bothered him, though, and he was earnestly trying to do the right thing.

Not long after his prayer, Bradley and his wife were sitting in a restaurant when one of these women from his past walked in with her partner. They sat in the booth next to him and his wife. Bradley's wife decided to go to the salad bar, got up, and walked off. Sure enough, the woman's partner did the exact same thing, leaving her and Bradley facing each other across the booths.

She got up, walked over to his table and said to him, "My friend doesn't know about us. Please don't say anything or recognize me." Then she went back and sat down.

Bradley realized that this was how God had let forgiveness take place. He was willing to confess his wrongful past if necessary, but in that instance it would not have been appropriate. He accepted God's provision, becoming free of the responsibility to share their past with anyone else. To go on from there and insist on confessing this sin regardless of what the friend or his wife thought would have been very damaging. God knew he was willing to make it right, and he was able to clear his conscience.

When I was a pastor, I once got into an argument with a fellow pastor about a certain issue. He made me mad and I said some pretty mean things to him. I was clearly in the wrong. Much later, as I was dealing with my bitterness and clearing my conscience, the Holy Spirit brought this incident to mind. I had no idea where this brother was, but I knew I had never made it right. So I just prayed, "Lord, if it's important for me to see this pastor that I said these things to, bring him back into my life in a very special way."

You can probably guess what God did. I was at a pastors' conference, sitting in the coffee shop. A friend came in with a gray-haired man and introduced him to me. It was this pastor I had prayed about. I didn't recognize him. I almost dropped my teeth. Almost—this was back in the days before I could actually do that!

I was so stunned that I just mumbled something and left. Later that day I went walking around the conference grounds, telling myself how incredible it was that God had brought this man back into my life, just like I prayed. I was so excited about the chance to go back and set things right with him.

That night at dinner I didn't see him, so I asked where he was. "Oh," someone said, "his church called and he had to go home today." Obviously, I had waited a little too long to seek him out.

Now, this wasn't a life-or-death situation, and I doubt if this man's future depended on it. But what I did was wrong, and I learned a very valuable lesson from it. It was as if God said to me, "Jim, when you purpose in your heart to get right with somebody, you'd better duck because I'm going to bring him back into your life if it's important, and you need to be ready to act." When God provides you such an opportunity, if the time is right and privacy between you and the other person exists, by all means sit down and seek his or her forgiveness.

Letting Go of the Past

If we don't keep our conscience clear, the enemy gains an advantage over us. That seems clear in the judgment inflicted on Hymenaeus and Alexander in 1 Timothy 1:19–20. A clear conscience before God is absolutely essential for us as Christians. In fact, Paul wrote that the "end of the commandment"—that is, the purpose of ministry or the purpose of our teaching—is love that flows "out of a pure heart, and of a good conscience, and of faith unfeigned" (1 Timothy 1:5).

Do you want God's love to flow out of you to others? Then a clear conscience is one of the three essentials Paul mentions. I see an interesting progression here. A pure heart looks at the present, a clear conscience at the past, and genuine faith at the future. If your heart is pure and the past is taken care of, you can look to the future with assurance.

What would you think if you got into a car with me and I started driving down a busy street looking only in the rearview mirror? After you swallowed the lump in your throat, you'd probably say, "Jim, you're looking the wrong way!"

You're right; I can't go forward looking backward, and neither can you. But that's just where Satan wants us to look. Paul wrote that we should let go of the past (Philippians 3:13). You don't have to pretend it didn't happen. Just let it go.

The enemy wants you to dig up your past. But when you dig up something dead, guess what? It stinks. God says the past is buried and He will never bring it up again. It's under the blood of Christ.

When Paul says he forgot "those things which are behind," he didn't mean he tried to act as if the past never happened. The word means "to disregard the significance" of it. He put it away and moved on. When you let go of the past, you are free to reach out with both hands to receive what God has for you now. With a clear conscience you can look people in the eye, then go out and do great damage to Satan and his kingdom.

The Problem of Guilt

Whenever I talk about having a clear conscience and not allowing the enemy to torment us with the past, this question usually comes up: "What do you do when you have terrible memories you just can't handle?"

Excellent question. All of us suffer from the consequences of our sin, even after we're cleansed of that sin. One of sin's consequences is the scar left by painful memories. Another name for this is guilt. Satan loves to remind us of the things we've done so he can keep us in bondage to guilt. "Remember that awful thing you did? How can God use a person like you?"

Try to Forget It?

So we have these memories of things which we can't deny doing. But what do we usually tell people who are struggling with the guilt of past sins? Forget it, don't think about it.

I often ask my counselees, "Does it help to try and forget it?"

"No, it makes it worse. The more I try not to think about it, the more I think about it."

They're right. Have you ever tried not to think of something? It doesn't work, does it? We saw above that putting the past behind you doesn't mean trying to forget it or pretend it never happened.

Thank God for the Memory

I encourage people to deal with guilt this way. First I ask them, "Who was in charge of your life when you made that wrong decision?"

HIGHER GROUND:
Having a Clear Conscience

Having a conscience free from guilt means clearing all offenses against others and, where possible, seeking forgiveness and making restitution. God is involved in this process, as shown below.

1. If someone you know was making a list of people who had hurt them and never asked their forgiveness, would you be on that list? Pray, asking God to reveal anyone who might feel you hurt them.

2. Make a list of all the people God brings to your mind whom you have offended and have not sought forgiveness from.

3. If possible, go over your list with a mature Christian and identify the basic offense against each person on that list. If you need to ask God's forgiveness for these offenses, do so now. It's always the right time to get right with God.

4. Rule out those people in whose lives your reappearance now would cause serious difficulty; for example, an old girlfriend who is now married.

5. Contact those individuals by telephone if possible, and be brief. Tell the particular person that as you have been looking back over your life, you realize that you failed him in _____ way, naming the offense. Then ask for forgiveness.

6. Make restitution where needed.

7. If certain people have benefited you but you've never shown appreciation, express to them gratitude for what you have gained. If you have a problem with being grateful, start sending thank-you notes to people who have benefited you, sharing how God has used them to build, strengthen, or challenge you.

8. Ask God to take back all ground given to Satan because you have purposed in your heart to contact these people and make things right.

"I was."

"Then instead of trying to forget or suppress the memory of that sin, do this. Whenever the enemy brings it to mind for the purpose of accusing you, face it and say, 'God, thank You for allowing me to remember what happens when I run my life. Right now, I want to rededicate my life to the Lord Jesus Christ. I want Him to sit on the throne of my life, because I know that when He runs my life, I won't do those kinds of things.'"

If guilt is a problem for you, I urge you to follow that simple formula. It's not a magic formula, nor is it automatic—but it can be very freeing. The enemy comes with these intruding thoughts to drive a wedge between you and God, to keep you from rededicating your life to God.

The only way I know to stop these thoughts is to thank God for the memory and dedicate yourself afresh to God. Many people have told me that after a period of doing this, the accusing thoughts stopped.

Be Like Paul

By the way, I'm not the first person to use this idea. I believe this is exactly what Paul did when Satan reminded him of his dark past.

And did Paul ever have a past. Think about the memories he had to deal with. He spent his time before conversion rounding up Christians and having them put to death (Acts 22:4). I can imagine him going somewhere to preach and having some believer say, "Oh yes, I know who you are. You're the one responsible for my grandmother's death."

Paul never forgot what he did to the church, but look at how he handled those memories. We have at least three examples in his writings, in 1 Corinthians 15:9; Ephesians 3:8; and 1 Timothy 1:12-15. Turn to each of those texts and you'll see that while Paul frankly acknowledges his past actions, he turns those painful memories into occasions of praise and thanksgiving to God for the abundant grace He bestowed on Paul. We would do well to imitate the apostle's example.

The Issue of Rebellion

Now I want to move into another key area where we can yield a tremendous amount of ground to Satan and give him a huge advantage over us if we're not walking in obedience to the Lord. The immediate aftermath of King Saul's disobedience is described in 1 Samuel 15:22–23. The prophet Samuel reproved Saul for his serious act of disobedience and then told him, "Rebellion is as the sin of witchcraft."

Rebellion and Witchcraft

That's a remarkable statement. God, speaking through His prophet Samuel, is telling us that if a person goes into rebellion, He regards it as similar to the sin of witchcraft, or "divination" as some translations put it. But how does rebellion resemble witchcraft? And what implications does this truth have for us today as we seek to walk in the victory Christ has secured for us over Satan and his ways?

First, it's clear that you can't practice witchcraft without opening yourself up totally to the control of Satan and his demons. In fact, witchcraft brings a person in direct contact with the demonic world without any kind of protection in between. Those who have been in that horrible practice will tell you that when you venture into Satan's kingdom, you are at his mercy. There's nothing to protect you from his attacks.

Losing God's Protection

So how does an awful sin like witchcraft compare to the sin of rebellion? In this way: when we rebel against God's constituted authority, we step out from under His protection and leave ourselves wide open to the attacks of the enemy. I once asked my Sioux Indian friends, "If a fort was under attack by the Sioux, which side of the walls would I want to be on?" They all said the inside, of course. But rebellion puts me on the outside, where I'm completely vulnerable. In other words, what we are dealing with here is the issue of God's authority. Another word for authority is *protection*. God has established authority structures which provide us with spiritual protection when we are in proper submission to them.

One of these God-ordained authority structures is the church. That's why, as we saw earlier, church discipline is the process of removing a person from the protection of the church and turning him or her over to demons to be tormented and brought to repentance. Family and government are two more structures which are also designed by God to give us spiritual protection. We should submit to their authority in our lives.

You may not like a lot of what's happening in our government. I'm not thrilled with it either. But if you've ever been in a country when the government was being overthrown, you'll discover real fast that government is better than anarchy.

I was in Nigeria when an attempted coup occurred. One day everything was fine. The next day, the streets were full of soldiers and tanks. There was a complete information blackout, so no one knew what was going on. It was a horrible experience. I was very scared. We were totally at the mercy of those troops. Let me tell you, government is better than anarchy because an organized, respected government provides protection.

Biblical concepts like authority, submission, and obedience are not popular today. That's more an indictment of our age than a legitimate criticism of Scripture. But we should not question the importance of authority and obedience. Consider the family. An authority structure there is clearly God's plan—the way He designed the family to work. We cannot dodge, deny, or ignore His clear teaching on authority without paying the price.

Make no mistake about it. A family where the children are living in obedient submission to their parents; where the wife helps her husband, sharing her input and wisdom with him and then supporting him in his decisions; and where the husband is in turn living in obedient submission to God is not some outdated arrangement. It is God's plan, and He expects us to line up under His structure of authority.

Heading Straight Down

The consequences for disregarding or disobeying authority are so sure and so devastating that we cannot afford them any longer in our own families or in the family of God. He will not tolerate rebellion. What happens when you or I rebel? When I rebel, I move out from under God's protection. Now what's between me and the forces of evil? Nothing! Demonic spirits have direct access to me. This is how rebellion is like witchcraft, because in witchcraft a person attempts to make direct contact with spirits.

If you've been on one of those really wild rollercoasters, you know you don't have to ask when it's time to scream. Everything is going along fine for a few moments, then suddenly the car takes a plunge and you're on your way down.

That's how it is with rebellion. Have you ever seen a rebel draw closer to God? No, he moves away from God. A boy rebels against his parents, and for a time nothing seems to happen. Then he hits that certain point, and from there it's downhill all the way. That rebel is in for a frightening ride, and I've seen some real tragedies come into the lives of rebels.

Foolishness, Disobedience, and Rebellion

Rebellion is serious and needs to be treated seriously. But I've had parents confuse rebellion with foolishness. They bring their kids to me and say, "Mr. Logan, my child is rebellious." When I talk to the son or daughter, however, I discover they aren't really rebellious at all. That's why I think it's so helpful with parents to distinguish among foolishness, disobedience, and rebellion. They're not the same.

Suppose a neighbor boy comes over to your house, picks up your son's ball, and says, "Here, catch." So the kids start playing ball in the house and they break a lamp. That's *foolishness.* You may need to apply some discipline for breaking the lamp, but the root of the problem was not rebellion.

Suppose the same kid comes over the next day and says, "Let's play catch." Your son says, "Oh, no. My dad says we can't play ball in the living room."

"Come on, just once," the other kid says. So your son throws the ball and it breaks a lamp.

That's *disobedience.* You told him not to do it, and he did it.

Now suppose the same neighbor kid shows up again the third day and the same conversation takes place. Your son refuses to play ball in the living room because his dad said so. Only this time the other boy replies, "Your dad has no right to tell you what to do."

That's *rebellion.* It's challenging the right of an authority to be there. Who gave fathers their authority? God did, so when children challenge a dad's authority they are really challenging God.

God's Authority Figures

Romans 13:1–4 deals with the authority God has established:

Let every soul be subject unto the higher powers. For there is no power but of God: the powers that be are ordained of God. Whosoever therefore resisteth the power, resisteth the ordinance of God: and they that resist shall receive to themselves damnation. For rulers are not a terror to good works, but to the evil. Wilt thou then not be afraid of the power? do that which is good, and thou shalt have praise of the same: for he is the minister of God to thee for good. But if thou do that which is evil, be afraid; for he beareth not the sword in vain: for he is the minister of God, a revenger to execute wrath upon him that doeth evil.

Paul says authority figures are God's ministers. Of course, he's talking about the office here and not necessarily the person. What about a person who is in an authority structure that is dangerous? He or she needs to be removed and placed under another authority.

We can't let a child, for example, be continually sexually abused by someone in authority. In that case we try to move the child into a different authority structure, but not take her out from under authority altogether. Why? Because authority is protection, and we need as much spiritual protection as possible.

First Timothy 2:1–4 tells us to pray for all of those in authority. The only thing that will make a difference in the leadership of our country is prayer. Instead of running our leaders down, we need to run them up!

Ephesians 6:1–3 is vital truth for children and teenagers. For years I had basically skipped over the first half of verse 3, which says children should obey and be respectful so that "it may be well with [them]." You know what that means? If children and teens are not obeying their parents, it is God's responsibility to see that things don't go well for them. God honors His Word!

If you're a parent, you can help your children in growing up by teaching them obedience and respect. Remember that there are two sides to this thing. *Obedience* is an action, *honor* is an attitude. Honor means respect, and children need to be disciplined for being disrespectful. The child who snarls, stomps off, and slams the door behind him when he's asked to clean up his room needs to be brought back for an attitude tune-up. Why? Because where there is dishonor, there will soon be disobedience. We always tried to discipline our kids at the attitude and character stage before it came to the action stage.

What if an authority asks children to do something in clear violation of the teaching of God's Word? Then they need to appeal with a respectful attitude. Our four children often had to stand alone for biblical principles in the public schools. Our oldest daughter, Cheryl, was the shiest of all the kids. In high school, she was in a choir that was ranked all-state. The problem was, her choir was planning to sing the song "Aquarius," a 1960s' hit that says we get our guidance from the stars.

Cheryl came to me and said, "Dad, I can't sing this song. What should I do?"

"Why don't you stand on your principles and appeal to authority?" I said. "Tell your choir director how much you appreciate all you've learned in choir, but you don't feel you can sing this song because you're a Christian."

She was really scared, but she did it. The choir director became so angry he told her to get out. She came home crushed. At the next practice she was very nervous. The director got up and said, "Someone has a problem with one of the songs we're singing, and we don't have time to learn another one. How many of you would prefer not to sing 'Aquarius'?" Every hand went up, the leader dropped that song, and my daughter floated home!

The Sad Result of Rebellion

Unfortunately, not all the testimonies I have on file in the area of rebellion and authority end so happily. Several years ago Stuart, a

HIGHER GROUND:
Rebellion

1. Ask God to forgive you for not submitting to the authorities He has placed in your life.

2. Purpose in your heart to get under all the proper authorities in your life, whether God, the church, the government, your parents, your husband, an educational institution, or your employer.

3. Ask forgiveness of the authorities you have rebelled against and tell them that with God's help, you will submit to them. Enlist their prayer support where that is appropriate.

sixteen-year-old, came to my office. He was deeply into homosexuality and was practicing Satanism. He describes his attitudes and actions to his father and God:

> At the age of 13, I began listening to both Christian and secular rock and roll and heavy metal music. These avenues allowed Satan to blind my spiritual sight so that I quickly became rebellious. I came to the point where I hated my dad and all he stood for. In fact, I hated him so much that I wanted to kill him. I also killed God in my mind. I blamed Him for the demonic attacks on me and for the upheaval I was causing in my family. I had many battles with my dad, trying to usurp his authority over our home. Those years contained much turmoil and grief for all of us.
>
> Just before my 16th birthday, seeing that my dad was relinquishing no authority . . . I left home to become my own boss.

Stuart was deeply rebellious, but it was obvious he didn't want to do anything about it. He left my office in rebellion and plunged more deeply into homosexuality and other perversions—and within less than two years had contracted HIV.

God finally broke through to him, and he surrendered his life to Christ. He's now back home living under his father's authority and they're studying the Word together. But this young man still suffers the consequences of his rebellion. HIV continues to threaten his health.

Stuart called me not long ago and I had a very touching conversation with him and his father. The timing of his call was of God, because the very next week I counseled another sixteen-year-old who was making the same decision to live a homosexual lifestyle. I asked Stuart if he would tell his story to this teenager, and he agreed.

I made the call in my office, handed the teenager the receiver, and left so they could talk privately. I was so excited because I just knew Stuart's testimony would turn this young teen around. As his godly parents sat in our lobby weeping, the kid listened to the testimony of a guy who never thought he would contract HIV, now living with the virus. As Stuart told him, he got the virus because he wanted to be his own boss.

They talked for more than an hour, yet when I went back in this teenager said, "That has no relevance to me." He hung up the phone, and he's still living in rebellion and perversion today.

Rebellion is something every teenager has to deal with. Every young person needs to answer the question, Who is going to be the final authority in my life?

For a lot of the adults I counsel, rebellion is something that was in the past and has been dealt with. In these cases they may need to ask God to take back the ground they yielded in rebellion.

Wherever we are on the spectrum, all of us need to place ourselves under the authorities God has put over us. Even if these authorities are not perfect, and none of them are, they provide us with spiritual protection from direct demonic attacks.

— 6 —
WHAT'S SO
TERRIBLE ABOUT PRIDE?

In my week-long counseling sessions with people who are under the influence of the enemy, there's usually a major turning point. The neon light goes on and begins to flash the shiny word: pride.

They realize that pride has become the source of the problem, the base from which Satan has been able to launch his attacks. Even though the counseling sessions have not yet dealt directly with the enemy's influence in the person's life, the problem of pride becomes obvious. That's how important the issue of pride is.

The Original Sin

Sometimes we forget: pride was the original sin in God's universe. Before Adam and Eve were ever created and placed in the Garden of Eden, the angel Lucifer, who stood in the very presence of God, allowed his heart to swell with pride at his exalted position. His pride led him into foolish rebellion as he tried to usurp the throne of God. Is it any wonder then that the one who became Satan would use pride as one of his most effective weapons? As we begin to see how pride opens us up to Satan's influence, we must look at pride's origin—among the angels in heaven itself!

Pride originated in heaven, and we can see this by looking at Ezekiel 28:11–19. Bible scholars debate whether this passage, and Isaiah 14 as well, refer to Satan or to human rulers. But notice that Ezekiel changes his reference from "prince" (28:2) to "king" (28:12), using both different Hebrew words and issuing different indictments in the two verses. The prince of verses 2–10 is judged because he, though a mere man, tried to be like God. But the exalted language of verses 11–19 cannot be ascribed to a mere human. Verses 11–15 describe the beauty of Satan before his fall. As the prince of angels, he was covered with a robe of precious stones, and light came from him.

The revelation of Satan's transgression is found in verse 17: "Thine heart was lifted up because of thy beauty." The prophet Isaiah makes the picture even clearer when he declares, "How art thou fallen from heaven, O Lucifer, son of the morning" (14:12). Isaiah then recounts Satan's five "I will" statements showing this dark angel's prideful rebellion against God.

A Sin of the Heart

Whenever I read this with those I counsel, I always ask them, "Who was Lucifer speaking to when he said these things?" The inevitable answer is that he was talking to God.

But then I have them read it again. Satan made his pride statements not to God, not even out loud necessarily, but *in his heart* (v. 13). God judged Satan for the thoughts of his heart, because as a person thinks in his heart, "so is he" (Proverbs 23:7).

The Bible says this repeatedly, by the way. If you want to do a fascinating Bible study, get a Bible concordance and look up every reference to what we say in our hearts. You'll be amazed at what you find.

I'm convinced that real and lasting change will never be made in people's lives until they change the way they think. Remember, the strongholds the enemy builds in our lives are constructed on lies. These lies are repeated so often that we come to believe and act on them. That's why part of spiritual warfare is tearing down these strongholds.

The last of Satan's "I will" claims recorded in Isaiah 14 is the most important for our purposes. "I will be like the most High" (v. 14). Why, out of all the names for God that Satan could have used, did he choose this one? "The most High" is a translation of *El Elyon,* which literally means "the sovereign one who reigns," or "the one who reigns sovereignly in heaven and on earth."

What Satan was saying here is that he wanted to be like God in control, but not in character. He wanted to rule. He wanted to run his own life. Satan's rebellion was a creature-centered movement, just like the New Age is today.

The Worst Sin

Do you see why pride is so repugnant to God? Do you see why it's the worst sin anyone can commit? It's like waving a fist of rebellion in the face of the Ruler of the universe.

When you attempt to run your own life, when you say, "God, You rule heaven, I'll rule me," you are most like Satan.

It's vital that we see the sin of pride for what it is and what it does. A quick run-through of Proverbs reveals God's attitude and response to pride. If we begin at Proverbs 6:16–17, we find this devastating pronouncement: of the seven sins God hates most, pride is at the top.

"The fear of the Lord is to hate evil," according to Proverbs 8:13. And in Proverbs 6:17 the very first evil listed is pride: the haughty eyes reflect both arrogance and pride. In fact, this verse can be translated to mean that God hates pride and arrogance as much as an evil lifestyle.

Why is that? What's so terrible about pride? It is setting you and me up as the final authorities in our lives, deciding for ourselves what's right and wrong for us. That's taking God's place in our lives, and He hates it.

But the Proverbs have a lot more to say. "When pride cometh, then cometh shame" (11:2). Notice the text doesn't say exactly how this happens, but the link between the two is inescapable. Proverbs 13:10 says, "Only by pride cometh contention." Ever had any contention in your home or church? We all have. At its root is pride.

Proverbs 15:25 is a warning to families: "The Lord will destroy the house of the proud." Interestingly, many teenagers who are angry at their fathers ask me two common questions: "Why is he always angry?" and "Why won't he ever admit he's wrong?" The teenagers resent their fathers' attitude, and many rebel because "Dad acts like he's always right and has to do things his way." Sadly, many fathers think that if they admit they're wrong, they will lose face before their kids.

What fathers don't realize is that if they refuse to admit they're wrong, they've lost face with their children already. Pride builds walls between people, but those walls have to come down because God says He will destroy the house of the proud. He's not talking about a physical building here, but a family. There's a Bible promise you'll never hear in a praise meeting!

"Every one that is proud in heart is an abomination to the Lord" (Proverbs 16:5). Abomination is one of the hardest and strongest words in the Old Testament. An abomination is something detestable and repulsive. One of the most famous Proverbs on pride is 16:18: "Pride goeth before destruction, and an haughty spirit before a fall."

And finally, Proverbs 29:23 says that "a man's pride shall bring him low." Every one of these verses is worthy of more study, but I wanted to give you a sense of how seriously God views pride, and how categorically the Bible denounces it.

Dealing with Pride

How does all of this happen? How can pride enter a person's life and bring such destruction? And how do we deal with this sin? Thankfully, the dynamics of how this works are explained for us in the book of James, which is the Proverbs of the New Testament. I guarantee you that if you can get hold of the truth we're about to consider, it can turn your life around.

For an example of humility, which is the opposite of pride, consider the author of the book of James. As the half-brother of the Lord Jesus Christ, James could have touted his relationship in his letter to Christians. When you and I know somebody important, sometimes we're tempted to do just that. By the way, did you know I had lunch in Washington along with the president one day? I did. I ate lunch in Washington one day and the president was somewhere in town eating lunch too, I'm sure.

But in the opening words of the book of James, the apostle wrote with humility. He did not start out, "James the half-brother of Jesus. You'd better listen to what I'm saying." Instead, James identifies himself simply as a servant of Christ. He realized his purpose was to serve, not to win praise or attention. So we know that when James gets ready to talk about pride and humility we need to listen, because he obviously possessed humility.

"More Grace"

The antidote to pride is recognizing God's grace. Knowing His gift to us, we realize that in ourselves we have little to offer. Instead, we respond in humility to His graciousness. Interestingly the apostle wrote that God gives "more grace" (4:6). Isn't that great? Which do you want, grace or "more grace"? The problem is, if God is going to give me more of it, what is grace? I find that many Christians don't really know what it is.

Many of us accept that definition of grace as the "unmerited favor of God." But His love and mercy are unmerited too. I think we need a definition of grace that takes us beyond that. We can't find salvation without grace. We need grace for spiritual warfare. We need grace for spiritual victory. But what is grace?

If you're a follower of Christ,' God is working in your life right now, according to Philippians 1:6. Remember, as Christians you and I are people in progress. God is actively working in two ways, according to Philippians 2:13. He is working in us "both [1] to will and [2] to do of his good pleasure." This means God is giving me both the desire and the power to please Him. That's what grace is.

So when God promises to give us more grace (James 4:6), He is offering more desire and more power than what we need. Then do we need to fear the enemy and his assaults?

Not at all. As we'll see in a later chapter, when we're in God's will He builds a hedge of protection around us. The only way the enemy can get at us with his temptations is with God's permission. And God will give us "more grace" to respond to those temptations victoriously.

The Reason for Defeat

If all this power is available for us to live victorious Christian lives, you may ask, "Why are there so many losers on the winning team? Why is the church full of so many defeated Christians? Why are so many youth groups plagued by the same sins that mark unbelieving young people?" Many rightly ask those questions, and they may even wonder, though they wouldn't ask it out loud, *Has God failed us?*

What's the problem? Pride. When we let pride come into our lives, God withholds spiritual power. And as we read in Proverbs, after pride comes a fall. The enemy brings in a destructive temptation which is too strong for us to handle, and without God's power we fall.

It makes sense, doesn't it? Look at the second half of James 4:6. "Wherefore he saith, 'God resisteth the proud, but giveth grace unto the humble.'" This is the reverse of Romans 8:31, which says, "If God be for us, who can be against us?"

That's a great verse, but think about what the opposite of it must mean. If God is resisting you, does it make any difference who is for you? When I see that word *resist,* I picture a big arm coming out of heaven, keeping me away from fellowship. And sin does that.

When Satan succumbed to pride, God shoved him out of heaven. When I allow pride in my life, God shoves me away, as it were. He says, "I'll take My power off of your life." What will happen then? I'll fall.

That's why as long as we allow pride in our lives, it's all over spiritually for us. It's just a matter of time until we fall. Pride precedes a fall. But God gives grace to the humble person, the one who says, "Lord without your empowering, I can't do it. If you don't give me your strength for today, I'm not going to make it. Lord, I need you."

Submitting to God

A key part in dealing with pride is found in this divine order: "Submit yourselves therefore to God. Resist the devil, and he will flee from you" (James 4:7). It's not hard to understand this command with a promise. The key is in the first three letters of the word *submit:* "Sub" means to rank under.

We submit to God, and from the place of submission to Him we are ready to resist. Submission is the first thing we have to do to be

HIGHER GROUND:
Dealing with Pride

1. Identify the key areas of your life such as work, finances, reputation, friends, entertainment, and future choices (marriage, etc.). Place all of these on the altar as an act of your will, praying, "God, I want to place all the areas of my life under Your control. I truly want to say with Paul, 'For me to live is Christ.'"

2. In 1 Corinthians 15:31 Paul says, "I die daily." Every day, make a conscious decision to die to self and be committed to God's will and purpose for your life.

3. Memorize Luke 9:23; Galatians 2:20-21; and 1 Corinthians 15:31.

4. Ask God's forgiveness for the areas of your life you have built around self, and surrender them to God. Ask Him to take back any ground you have surrendered to Satan.

successful in spiritual warfare. That usually means a battle with pride right off, because it's not natural for human beings to relinquish control of their lives to anyone else. It can only be done supernaturally.

Resisting Satan

Notice that we are not ready to resist Satan's approach until we submit to God. People tell me all the time, "Oh, I tried to resist Satan, but it doesn't work." That's just the problem. We cannot "work" it ourselves. We have to work it on God's terms. If we're prideful, guess what? The devil isn't going anywhere.

We have to understand that we don't have a better idea. We've got to get our lives under what God says. Then we'll have the benefit of what He promises.

A good question to ask yourself is, *Am I willing to submit to God in every area of my life, to rank myself under His authority?* If not, you'll experience constant defeat in your attempts to resist Satan. It's vital that you see this. It could turn the whole battle for you. I ask my counselees to make a list of any area where they're having trouble submitting to God, and then release these areas to Him.

In chapter 13, we'll deal more fully with this all-important subject of resisting Satan. One reason it's so important is that I have discovered Christians who have never, to their knowledge, resisted Satan even once!

Following God's Plan

I'm not suggesting that resisting Satan or submitting to God is always easy. I admit it—sometimes, it's hard for me to say no to myself and my will and yes to God. Why is it so difficult? Because my ways are not God's ways (see Isaiah 55:8).

Sometimes I say to myself, and sometimes to God, "I know your ways are not like mine. I wish they were." You see, I know that God's ways are different than my ways—and obviously a whole lot better and wiser. But it's still a struggle for me to get under God's authority. Sometimes, God wants me to do things that I don't think I want to do.

I remember one particular struggle so well. I had accepted God's call to minister to missionaries, but I didn't want to go to India. I had heard all the horror stories about conditions over there. *There's no way I can handle it,* I told myself. *There are beggars rolling in the dirt, no place to go to the bathroom, no safe drinking water . . .* On and on I went, complaining, doubting, resisting.

So I went to Africa instead. When I got there, guess what I encountered? Beggars rolling in the dirt, no place to go to the bathroom, no safe drinking water. Dumb me! After that I realized I could go to India after all.

We've all had those struggles, those wrestling matches with the Lord to get our will underneath His in submission. I'm glad in my case that God has won His share. I'm thankful He won in those times when His will didn't look appealing or didn't even look like the right thing to do at the moment. I knew the problem wasn't what God was asking me to do. What He really wanted was for me to bring my will under His authority. If I didn't, I knew I would be defeated.

There's one thing I learned early on in my counseling ministry: this kind of ministry can humble you very quickly. There are times I just walk up and down the hall in our offices saying, "God, I don't know what to do. There's a person in my office who is being tormented and I don't know what to do. I've tried everything."

That's humbling, let me assure you. But I thank God for what those experiences teach me. Many times my colleagues and I get together in our offices and pray, "Lord, we don't know what to do. We want to help this person, but we don't know how to do it. Show us what to do."

Who's in Charge?

So we come back again to the one great battle we all have to fight: who is going to be the final authority in my life? Am I going to hold on to the throne of my heart in stubborn pride, or I am going to let the Lord Jesus be Lord of my life?

You know, it's amazing how closely authority and power are linked in Scripture. You're either under God's authority, living in submission to Him, or you're resisting Him. If you are resisting God in any area in your life, you will not have the strength you need to resist the enemy.

My Way or God's Way

If pride is such a lethal problem for us, maybe we should ask how we can get rid of it. I think you know the answer to that. We cannot. We can never simply rid ourselves of pride once and for all—we never will as long as we're in this body. Pride is allowing self to sit on the throne of my life instead of Christ. It's building life around my will instead of God's will. But we can deal with our pride, as Jesus tells us in Luke 9:23. The answer is you and I must deny self. Whenever someone says to me, "I'm just trying to find myself," my reply is, "When you find it, crucify it."

Jesus said we must take up our cross daily and follow Him. I see the cross here in a very general way as God's will and purpose for my life. It's a decision we need to make every day of our lives. As the apostle Paul did, we must act in light of the truth that when we are crucified with Christ, it is Christ who lives in us and empowers us, and we live "by faith in the Son of God, who loved [us] and gave himself for [us]" (Galatians 2:20).

I request those I counsel to write Luke 9:23 on a card and put it on their bathroom mirror or somewhere so that they see it every day and are reminded of the decision they have to make. I encourage you to do the same. It makes for a healthy, balanced life, one in which Christ is in control and we submit to His leadership. There is little room for Satan in such a life.

When we try to regain control of the reins of our lives, eventually pain follows. No one is immune. I get calls all the time from people who have lost their ministries, and in some cases are facing jail, because at some point they made the decision to do what they wanted to do.

Jesus goes on to say in Luke 9:24, "For whosoever will save his life shall lose it: but whosoever will lose his life for my sake, the same shall save it." There are really only two ways: your way, and God's way. You've got to decide which it will be. I pray that you will learn to deal with pride and let it go.

— 7 —

BREAKING THE SHACKLES
OF SEXUAL BONDAGE

Of the people who come to see me for counseling, about 90 percent are men. And of these men, the great majority are in some form of sexual bondage.

Yes, Satan is behind much of the sexual bondage in society. That does not mean that men and women are off the hook for their actions; you can't say, "The devil made me do it." But we must recognize that when we allow Satan to get a foothold in our lives, this is one key area in which he will attack us, especially as men. The enemy desires to wipe out men as leaders in the home and in the church. Yet I've seen exciting results as God enables many men to come to freedom in Christ. My files are full of wonderful testimonies from these men, but due to the nature of their problems I can't share a lot of them publicly. Those in this chapter, therefore, are only a handful, but they reflect the power of God active in many lives to overcome sexual bondage. (Of course, all names have been changed.)

Before looking at their lives and the deliverance they found, please note that most testify to feeling that their situations were hopeless. The enemy can build tremendously powerful strongholds in our lives when we believe and act as if there's nothing that can be done about our problem.

Remember what a stronghold is? It's a mindset impregnated with hopelessness that causes me to accept as unchangeable something that I know is contrary to the will of God. Once I believe there's no hope for me to change, I only have two choices. Either I give myself over to the sin, or I give up and try to take my life.

A Widespread Problem

I never speak anywhere—Christian or secular college campuses, churches, retreats—that I don't find men who are in bondage to sexual sin. It's so easy for men to be trapped by the lust of the flesh.

But this is not just a chapter for men. Our permissive society has now made it seem acceptable for women to pursue every possible sexual perversion too. I recently got a call from a national ministry to young people on college campuses. The caller said that many of the young women coming to Christ had become involved in sexual perversion while living in the dormitories.

This ministry was wondering if we were also finding an increase in the number of women trapped in sexual perversion. (We were.) In all their previous years of ministry, they had never seen this problem in such proportion.

Even a woman who is not having a problem, however, can experience devastating effects from her husband's sexual sin. Guess what intruding thoughts the enemy attacks her with when she discovers her husband is into this stuff? "There must be something wrong with me. I must not be very attractive to him if he has to get his 'thrills' like this. He wouldn't be doing this if everything were OK with me. I must be a failure as a woman and a wife."

What a powerful attack on a woman, hitting her at her greatest point of identity and vulnerability. The most moving example of this is the wife of my friend Bill, the young man whose story I told you back in chapter 1. She also wrote down her testimony, which is in my files. Her words demonstrate how a husband's sin can devastate his wife too:

> When my husband was going through his struggles, I had struggles of my own. I assumed they were the responses my mind was having to the trauma that had come into our lives. It never occurred to me that I was being influenced by the enemy.
>
> First of all, I struggled with angry, violent thoughts toward our [five] children. I felt extremely guilty about such thinking. I was also scared I would carry out such temptations . . . . I explained my struggle to our pastor's wife, and we agreed I would call her anytime I thought it was necessary.
>
> The other area of struggle was with suicidal thoughts. At the very least, I had convinced myself that they would have to lock me up if my husband gave up trying to get better. It wasn't like I didn't know better. I had been a growing Christian for 20 years. . . . But it was not until we learned about spiritual warfare and how to effectively resist the enemy that anything changed. We are free. It's almost like being born again.

Like every satanic attack, the area of sexual bondage affects the family. Bill's sexual bondage undercut his wife's confidence and even made her feel suicidal, just as Bill felt. And as we will see in chapter 9, it had effects on their children as well. Bill had no idea such things were going on in his wife's heart, and surely did not think there would be consequences for his children. He thought everything else was fine and his battle with sexual temptation and confusion with his sexual identity was a private fight.

Springing the Trap

Let me show you several ways that Satan can spring his trap of sexual bondage. He can use people and experiences at almost any stage of life to ensnare us.

Friends and Acquaintances

Joe, a medical doctor, had grown up in a Christian family with his brothers. Joe lived a pretty sheltered life, and says that until the sixth grade he had little knowledge of sexual matters. But when Joe was eleven years of age, another boy introduced him to pornography and the practice of masturbation. They became lustful practices, and Joe stayed in bondage all through the rest of his childhood and early adulthood.

Joe thought getting married would solve his problems, so he married a lovely young woman who was active in Christian ministry and really used of God. But he discovered that marriage did not resolve his problem with lust. Joe's wife had no idea of what he was struggling with as he sank deeper and deeper in his sin.

By the time I met Joe at a conference where I was speaking to medical doctors, he had given up hope and was resigned to being in bondage. But he came to freedom along with a number of other doctors at that conference, using the principles of spiritual warfare I am sharing in this book.

When Joe went back to his church and told others how God had delivered him, he was surprised at the response. Men seemed to come out of the woodwork, admitting that they too were fighting a losing struggle against lust. They wanted to know how he found victory.

Some time later I was speaking and counseling at another week-long conference for doctors. Joe was there, so I asked him if he would give his testimony of how God set him free. He asked his wife if it was all right with her, since she would be sitting in the meeting. He didn't want to embarrass her. But she agreed, so Joe and another doctor told about how God set them free of their bondage.

Experiences before Conversion

Sitting in the audience was a doctor I'll call Mike. *None of this is relevant to me because I would never fall victim to sexual bondage*, he thought. Mike reasoned that although he had been introduced to pornography at a young age and had allowed it to lead him into immoral episodes up through his college years, he had given his life to Christ at the age of twenty-one. Therefore, he told himself, since all of that other stuff happened before he was saved, and since he was now committed to Jesus Christ, it could never happen again.

It didn't happen for a while, to be sure. But a few years after this conference I got a call. The man on the other end of the line was sobbing. "Jim, help me." It was Mike. "I never would have dreamed that I would do what I've done. I've got serious sexual problems, and I'm afraid my wife is going to leave me. Please see me."

We made an appointment for a few months later. Mike came and was set free by the power of Christ. This doctor went home and shared these principles with his wife, and she came to freedom. His children were also having tremendous problems, including nightmares. When this father got his life squared away, he was able to help his kids.

Childhood Trauma

Let me give you more of Bill's story here. He came to my office a short time after he had left the Christian counseling center and hospital where they told him he would have to live with his identity as a sex addict and go to support groups for it. He was so distraught that he told me the only reason he didn't commit suicide was that he was afraid he would fail and be sent back there.

Bill's problems reached a long way back, to the earliest days of his childhood. He remembers being teased as effeminate in his first years in school, and feeling that the message he was receiving from the other boys was right: he was something other than a normal boy.

That was the beginning, but over the years Bill yielded more and more to these feelings until he reached the place where all hope seemed to be gone. These were not God's thoughts but intruding thoughts from Satan, as I showed Bill, for God calls us special and created as distinctively male and female. By believing the enemy's lie and acting on it, Bill had given Satan a foothold. Then, through repeated acceptance and acting out of Satan's intruding thoughts, Bill allowed Satan to build a towering stronghold of lies in his life, and he slipped deeper in sexual bondage.

When Bill came, we took back ground that he had yielded to Satan over many years. The thing that really broke it open for him was when we went through Romans 6 together, using a study technique that personalizes these verses.

Bill had some bitterness and a few other things, and we dealt with those too. But it was primarily the teaching of Romans 6 that helped him come to freedom. "I feel like something left me," he said.

Bill returned home and enjoyed several months of freedom, even though he told me the temptations were very intense at times. I told him that he would probably have what I call a real "defining moment" of temptation, when the enemy would let him have it with everything. Bill's defining moment did come, and it's described in chapter 14.

As of this writing, Bill has enjoyed more than two years of freedom. He even felt strong enough to come alongside me for a week as a prayer partner while I was counseling someone else.

A Road with No End

Here's a truth we all need to keep in mind. Sin and lust can never be satisfied. We just cannot get our fill to the point of satisfaction. A man once said to me in my office, "Mr. Logan, I need help. Even my perversions have become perverted." I didn't really catch what he was trying to say, so I asked him what he meant.

"Well, when I started I drew a line and said everything up to this line was OK. But the enemy pushed me over that line, so I drew another one. Now he's pushed me over so many lines I can't draw any more. I can't go any further into this sin than I've gone."

Sexual sin is like that. It can never satisfy, but it will always promise more if we participate more. And that's how Satan typically operates. Never content to leave us wading in the shallows of sin, he's always luring us deeper until we're way over our heads. By the time we realize we're in that deep, we can't swim back to shore.

And our bondage threatens to pull others in as well. Our children are sensitive to sin, and Satan's thoughts can attack them too, especially if Satan senses an opportunity. As a teenager, Carl found his dad's pornographic magazines and got hooked. "Where did you find them?" I asked him.

"Well," he said, "I just sort of pulled out the bottom drawer of my dad's dresser, and there they were on the floor inside the dresser."

Now, most teenagers don't go around checking under dresser drawers in their parents' bedroom. So I asked this young man, "What in the world made you do that?"

"I don't know. I just got this thought to look under there."

It doesn't take a brain surgeon to figure out who might have planted that thought in this teenager's mind. Satan specializes in that approach. Another teenager told me that as he was sitting on his dad's bed while they talked, he casually ran his hand between the mattress and box springs and felt a magazine. *I'll check this out later,* he told himself. He came back later, found his father's pornography, and got

HIGHER GROUND:
Leaving Sexual Bondage

Sexual bondage has trapped many men, but women increasingly are being lured by temptations in a sexually permissive society. In fact, sexual bondage is one of Satan's chief ploys in undermining the Christian. If you are enslaved by sexual bondage, here is a way to find freedom through Christ.

1. Ask God to reveal to you the first time you violated His moral law and began to give Satan ground in your life. In prayer, let God walk you through your life and acknowledge to Him all areas He brings to mind.

2. Confess anything that needs to be confessed and ask God to restore your fellowship with Him in that area.

3. Ask God to take back all ground given to the enemy through moral failure.

4. Dedicate your body to the purpose of bringing glory to God (1 Corinthians 6:19–20). Start with your thought life and end with your sexual desires. Pray, "God, I thank You that You made me with these drives. I surrender them to Your control."

5. Be on guard for the enemy to try and put you back under sexual bondage, and be ready to resist him (see chapter 13). Focus on the consequences of sin, not the pleasure.

6. Begin to memorize Scripture that you can use to resist the "bait" Satan will dangle in front of you to regain the ground you surrendered to God.

hooked. Think about it. You can't even get most teenagers to make a bed, let alone run their hand under the mattress!

I've warned audiences about sexual bondage and have repeated the stories of these two teens. A pastor came up to me after hearing the stories at one conference and said, "I've got to tell you my story.

"The same thing happened to me when I was a teenager," he began. "I ran my hand under my dad's mattress and felt a magazine. I thought it was pornography, so I pulled it out. It was *Holiness to the Lord.*" His father was a holiness pastor! Devoted to his faith, the man had kept the magazine close by, and his son had stumbled upon it. Wouldn't it be great if that's what all teens found underneath a dresser drawer or a mattress?

The "Romans Road" to Freedom

The path to freedom from sexual bondage is found on the Romans Road, particularly Romans 6. This is a marvelous chapter, and we use it regularly in our counseling; let me point out the key truths that spell release from sexual bondage.

Bad News, Good News

Reading only the first half of the verses as we go through Romans 6 shows the problem. Read the first half of each verse, and then go back and read the second half, and you will be able to draw out the implications—and the positive choice we can make.

For example, the first half of Romans 6:12 says, "Let not sin therefore reign in your mortal body." What picture does the word *reign* suggest to you? Most of my counselees will say, "A king on a throne."

That's an accurate picture. Consider what happens, then, if sexual sin is sitting on the throne of someone's life. The rest of the verse tells us: "that ye should obey it in the lusts thereof." A king is to be obeyed. Paul is not necessarily talking about just sexual lust here. Lusts are strong desires that can come in a number of areas. Whatever the problem, though, if it reigns over us, we must obey it.

Next, look at the first part of verse 13: "Neither yield ye your members as instruments of unrighteousness unto sin." I am to make a choice not to yield the members of my body to do unrighteous acts. Why? Because if I do, sin will dominate my life, and Paul tells us "Sin shall not have dominion over you" (v. 14a).

Look at verse 16: "Know ye not, that to whom ye yield yourselves servants to obey, his servants ye are?" What are the choices we have here? We can either serve sin, which leads to death, or serve righteousness. If I serve sin, I will become a slave to that which was once a choice. Slaves have no choices. Sin cuts us off from God, and the result is spiritual death. So when we live in bondage, we are cutting ourselves off from the very one who can help us. We're dead to God.

Soul Ties

What has happened is that our bond of fellowship with God is broken when we sin. Neil Anderson points out that in its place, people form all kinds of unnatural bondings. We call them "soul ties." A man who has relations with a prostitute bonds to that person, and the bond with God is broken (see 1 Corinthians 6:16).

These soul ties can be incredibly powerful. That's why a woman will go back time and again to a man who beats her. There's some kind of an unnatural tie to that person that has to be broken by the power of God.

After ice skater Tonya Harding won the U. S. figure skating championship in 1993 and her ex-husband was found to have been behind the attack on rival skater Nancy Kerrigan, people could not understand why Harding defended her former husband and even tried to reconcile with him. She had complained of beatings and had filed complaints. Yet despite his actions, she felt compelled to support him and even to return to him. Why? One reason might be that their sexual union had created strong bonds of identity and experience, bonds that could not easily be broken.

Remember what Proverbs 5:22 says? "He shall be holden with the cords of his sins." When Jesus raised Lazarus from the dead and he came out of the grave, he already had life. But he was still bound with his graveclothes, and he needed help getting unwound. There are people who have God's life in them, but they are bound up with all kinds of sins. Somehow, when it's sexual it seems to be worse.

The Lure of Eroticism

Romans 6:19 says that if I keep yielding my body to carry out sinful desires, it will lead me from iniquity to even deeper iniquity. What used to satisfy me doesn't satisfy anymore, and I need to go deeper into sin and become more twisted.

If you've never experienced sexual bondage, it's unlikely that you understand eroticism, which at its core is demonic. Eroticism is intense sexual pleasure beyond description that the enemy gives to keep a person in bondage. It just cannot be explained. As I talk to people who have these problems, they tell me that this is exactly what's happening. "The pleasure is so intense, so heightened that I can't explain it."

One man said just the thought of cross-dressing was a complete sexual pleasure experience. Another said that just driving around looking for someone to expose himself to gave him such overwhelming erotic feelings he couldn't describe them. He would drive for hours looking for someone.

Seeing the Truth

The perversion of such actions should be obvious. So I read the first half of Romans 6:21 with my counselees: "What fruit had ye then in those things whereof ye are now ashamed?" Then I'll ask the individual, "Aren't you ashamed?"

I remember one counselee's sad answer. "Oh, Mr. Logan, I'm so ashamed. When I think of all the evil I've done in yielding my body to sin, all the years I've let sin sit on the throne of my life, I'm so ashamed. I realize I'm in bondage."

When a person comes to the point of seeing that this is wrong, we stop there. It doesn't matter what the world thinks or who says it's all right. Many young men struggle with masturbation, yet even some Christian counselors say it's permissible. That kind of advice really messes these young men up. They do not dabble; they continue on, and it becomes an obsession that enslaves them. Or else it opens the door to serious perversion.

We have Christian young men who are being defeated many times a day through masturbation. That's not normal. I'm not saying this isn't a normal struggle that young men and women have to learn to deal with. But when it's out of whack, something is wrong.

It's like anger. Do teenagers get angry? Of course they do, but if your teenager is kicking holes in the wall, you have a suspicion that there's enemy involvement.

When I have kids in my office who are struggling with masturbation and constantly being defeated, I ask them if they're satisfied with that. Not one has said yes. They all want to be free of it. One teenager said to me, "If this is OK, how come I feel so awful about it?"

At this point the counselee and I pray together. In particular, we ask the Holy Spirit to show him or her when it was that they first gave ground to the enemy by violating God's moral standards.

For people who are in deep sexual bondage, this can go back a long way—much further than the people themselves would ever imagine. Many of these people began practicing sexual evil at incredibly early ages, long before they even understood what they were doing.

It doesn't make sense unless you understand these problems as what the Bible calls "iniquities," which are the sinful weaknesses of the fathers passed down through three and four generations. We'll talk about this in more detail in the next chapter. It's another very important concept you need to see.

The issue we're dealing with here is ground given to the enemy. So we pray and ask God to show the person every time he or she gave ground to the enemy that he is now using against them. We walk through the person's life until there's nothing left. Sometimes a counselee (like Dr. Mike whose story I told above) will object, "This happened before I became a believer." I remind them that the issue is ground they have yielded, which needs to be taken back.

Yielding to Christ

When this is done, we go back to Romans 6 and read the positive side of these verses. Then I ask the person to yield every member of his or her body as a servant to Christ (v. 13). This can be a struggle, because this is the first time most of these people have ever consciously committed their sexual parts, their sex drives, and the rest of their bodies to the Lord.

When we came to the point in Bill's counseling where he was to yield his sexual parts to God, things got very quiet. I knew his struggle, because a person with Bill's problem believes that God put him in the wrong body.

I cried out to God for Bill because I knew the battle raging in his spirit. Finally, he stammered as he thanked God for his sexual organs and thanked God that he was a man. At that moment the power of the enemy in his life was broken, and Bill was free. He had experienced the truth of Romans 12:1–2 and the freedom of 1 Corinthians 6:19–20.

The Temptation to Go Back

It should be no surprise that after a person has been delivered from the demonic powers of sexual bondage, temptations to renew that sin will still come, and come hard. We know the enemy doesn't give up anyone without a fight.

Selective Memory

And because Satan is both a liar and very clever, the temptation is always to the pleasure that this sin brought into the person's life. This is the most insidious thing about Satan's attacks. The person is tempted to remember the pleasure. But guess what he forgets about if he's not careful? The bondage that he—or she—was under when he enjoyed that pleasure.

This is the way sin works in all of us. When my oldest son was thirteen years old, I told him, "Richard, I want you to know something. Sin is pleasurable."

He said, "Oh, dad!"

I said, "Oh, yes! Read Hebrews 11:25. God says that sin is pleasurable for a season." I wanted him to realize that I was still in the real world. I understood that sin was pleasurable. But I also wanted him to know there's a huge price tag attached to sin.

In our ministry the biggest struggle with people who are in sexual bondage is that they remember the pleasure and not the chains that bound them. And there's a tremendous pull to go back and enjoy the pleasure. They need to learn to focus on the consequences of sin, not the pleasure. That's true for all of us. We have to ask ourselves, *Do I really want to give Satan victory over my life?*

It's like the children of Israel in the wilderness. They were tired of the same old menu—manna, manna, manna—and wanted to return to the leeks, onions, and garlic of Egypt. Somehow they forgot about the years of bondage to the Egyptians and recalled only the pleasure of tasty herbs and spices. "What's spaghetti without garlic?" they seemed to say. We may fault them, but in truth, pleasures of the flesh are tempting. We must remember they are also temporary and quite deceiving.

Fortifying our Hearts

How do you deal with the reality of sin's fleeting pleasure and the need to stand strong in the Lord? You need to get alone with the Lord and say, "Lord, what are my weak areas? Where are the areas in which I am most likely to yield to temptation?"

You may know already where you're weak. If not, the Holy Spirit will be faithful to reveal these things to you. Satan's chief tactic is to set a "snare" (2 Timothy 2:26), a trap he will use to lure us into doing his will.

Several years ago Mike, a hunter who enjoyed trapping many animals, invited me to join him one morning as he went to check his trap line. I was a pastor and after only a moment's hesitation said yes, knowing it's not every day a pastor is invited to hunt in the great outdoors. I nearly stepped in the first trap, because it was so well concealed all I saw was the hanging bait. The bait was appropriate for what this young man was trying to catch. If you want to catch a bear, you don't hang up a mouse.

We didn't catch a bear that day, but God impressed upon me an important point. Satan's traps are not only well hidden, but they are hung with just the right bait. You would be wise to identify the kind of bait Satan is most likely to use to trap you. Remember, he doesn't waste his time with temptations that don't have any appeal to you.

Scripture lists a number of these baits: the sensual woman (Proverbs 7:10-23), flattery (Proverbs 29:5), the fear of man (Proverbs 29:25), evil times (Ecclesiastes 12:9), pride (1 Timothy 3:6), the desire to be rich (1 Timothy 6:9), and opposing sound teaching (2 Timothy 2:25), just to name a few. Each of them can be an entry point for giving Satan a foothold in your life. Each can be the starting point to eventually yielding ground and sliding into sexual bondage. Again, ask God to show you where you are vulnerable. Once you've done that, I suggest that you get a Bible concordance and find scriptural truths that speak to your areas of weakness. After all, isn't the Word of God what we're supposed to use against the attacks of the enemy? Isn't it better to use a sword that fits you exactly than a sword that doesn't fit? Jesus defeated Satan using the Word of God. That's good enough for me!

— 8 —
FAMILIES
UNDER ATTACK

One facet of spiritual warfare is understood or accepted by few American families, yet it has an impact on families in Western cultures as surely as it does elsewhere. This is the area of family iniquities and ancestral spirits. As we look at ways Satan specifically attacks families, we must begin here.

If you have trouble accepting the idea that this stuff is real, you're not alone. When I was first learning about spiritual warfare—and remember, I didn't go looking for any of this—the hardest thing for me to accept was the idea that demons could transfer from one person to another or be passed down from generation to generation.

It's one of those areas where most Christians in the Western world would retreat to the argument that these things only happen in primitive, animistic cultures. That's about where I was at one time. It took a long time before I could say with conviction that I believed it because it didn't fit with conservative, fundamental Christianity.

As I said earlier, I'm a biblicist. If I'm going to believe and teach something, I have to see it clearly taught in the Bible. In my study I found that God warns about these things at least five times in His Word (see page 113), and I don't see where these teachings are limited to primitive cultures.

Two Case Studies

In this chapter we will look at those five instances in God's Word, but first let's look at a couple of case studies that attest to the reality. In my extensive work with Native Americans in this country and in Canada and with animistic people, my eyes have opened to the clear presence of the spirit world. We cannot ignore the Bible's warnings about such things as blessings and cursings and the "iniquities of the fathers being passed on to their children." Never have I seen this more clearly than while speaking at a series of meetings with Sioux tribespeople in South Dakota.

Old Spirits in South Dakota

During my week at the church sponsoring the meetings, a young believer, who we'll call David Mountain, told me about his grandfather, John Mountain, who had recently died. John Mountain had been the most powerful medicine man in the entire Sioux nation, possessing great spirit powers that he had inherited from his ancestors.

When John Mountain died, his spirits chose his son, the boy's father, to receive these powers. The father, Daniel Mountain, thus became a medicine man himself, although Daniel later told me that he had wanted his son David to take the grandfather's place. But since the son refused, Daniel had no choice but to receive the spirits himself.

So we had three generations here: the grandfather, who had been one of the most powerful Sioux medicine men; his son, the recipient of his father's spirits and powers and current medicine man; and the grandson, now a believer, who had refused the powers although hand-picked by his father for the role of medicine man.

This all came together for me at these meetings, because each night while we met, this medicine man held special meetings, (pronounced "U-weepy" by the Sioux), at which spirits would manifest themselves in strange ways. His purpose was to draw people away from our meetings.

David and other Christians at the church prayed with me each night that these demonic meetings would be interrupted by God. David's father finally called the missionary in whose church I was speaking and asked to meet with us. I was amazed to see that Daniel Mountain, this powerful medicine man, looked like an ordinary, well-dressed businessman.

We explained the way of salvation to him and spent about two hours explaining God's power over spirits. He told us more about John Mountain's death. When they carried John's coffin the one-and-a-half miles from the paved road to the burial place, fifty-five eagles had circled over the coffin. Now his father's spirits would come to Daniel at different times. He knew each time they were there because the room would fill with the fragrance of the cologne his father had worn. We explained that Christ had more power than these spirits and could set him free. We are still praying for his salvation.

I told you that David, this medicine man's son, had come to faith in Christ. At these same meetings I also met the medicine man's daughter, under rather strange circumstances. I was speaking in the church one night when I began to get a very strange feeling about a young woman who looked to be in her early twenties, sitting off to one side on the front row. The "vibes" coming from her were disturbing.

Now I'm not very sensitive to these things, so something has to be really powerful to get my attention. I didn't know who she was, but I remember thinking that something was not right here. After the service I learned her identity from the people in the church and found out this child of the medicine man had exhibited unusual powers since she was very young. At three years of age, she would go to her relatives' houses and levitate objects with her mind.

All of the people in the tribe had been afraid of this girl for years. Her own grandmother was so afraid of her she refused to let her into the house. The young woman came to the meetings we held. She says she is trusting the Lord for salvation, but it's very likely that she has not been set free from these ancestral spirits.[1]

A California Relative

In chapter 3, I mentioned my own family's involvement in the spirit world. You can go back and read the story again if you'd like. The place I left off was where my mother told me that the fortune-telling skills of my aunt living in California were taught to her by her mother, my grandmother.

In other words, the spirit that enabled my grandmother to "lay the cards" and read fortunes was passed on to her daughter. Now this woman and her daughter, my cousin, regularly practiced mental telepathy and at one time even considered opening a fortune-telling tea room.

Another intriguing thing my mother told me is that my grandmother on my father's side taught all her daughters to lay cards, but only this one daughter had the power to make it work.

Needless to say, all of this bothered me. One reason is that for about four years before she died, this grandmother lived behind us in our home in California. I would go to her house every day after school because my parents worked. Back then I considered her the one light in my life, because whatever I did was wonderful to her, and she would actually listen to me as I told her all about my day and the crazy things that go with being a teenager.

I was stunned when my mother told me about the powers my grandmother had and how she had passed them on to my aunt. As I said in chapter 3, I did some heavy-duty praying that none of this demonic influence would be passed on to our six grandchildren.

The Importance of Heritage

Things like this have nothing to do with getting into sin, but with heritage. I find it very interesting that the ancient church used to renounce Satan verbally at a person's baptism. Even today in many of the high liturgical churches, the baptismal prayers for children include a prayer renouncing the sins of their ancestors.

These familiar spirits pass down through families from generation to generation, and it still happens today. One area where I have seen this factor come into play in some dramatic ways is adoption.

The fact that a child was given up for adoption suggests that something is wrong. It's not normal for parents not to want their child. I realize there can be many possible scenarios in an adoption, and I'm sure there are many parents who would testify that their adopted boy or girl had a very normal childhood and is now a healthy, productive adult.

This is not meant to deny any of that. We can never limit the grace of God. What I'm talking about are adoptive families where things are not going well at all and there doesn't seem to be any explanation for the problem. My point is this. More often than not, a child who is put up for adoption is coming from a troubled family background. I think that much is safe to assume. In situations like these, family iniquity, what the Bible calls "the iniquity of the fathers," can definitely have an influence on the child.

We know this happens on the physical level. There are "crack" babies born to cocaine addicts who come into the world addicted to crack and have to suffer through withdrawal. The same is true for some babies born to alcoholics. We shouldn't be surprised when children born to spiritually sick people show the effects of their heritage.

One reason we need to consider this possibility is that few adoptive parents know the full family history of their child. When I say we can assume that an unwanted child is coming from a troubled family, I'm not just thinking of the immediate circumstances that led to the adoption: an unwed teen mother, for example. There may be, and often is, much more to the story.

I've dealt with so many of these cases that whenever a family calls me and describes a child whose behavior is beyond normal disobedience or out of control, the first question I ask is whether the child is adopted. I would say that half of the time, the answer is yes. It just reinforces the fact that a birth family has a great influence on a child.

In a village in Brazil, for instance, a tiny girl was brought to a local hospital from a brothel by one of the prostitutes. Maria was born to a prostitute and had lived in the brothel for all of her two or three years.

But she became very sick, so she was brought to the hospital. It turned out she had leukemia.

The nursing staff fell in love with and unofficially "adopted" Maria, since she was too sick to go back to the brothel. But they were stunned at how emotionally hardened she was. For a long time, no one could get through to her. Thankfully, a Christian nurse showed Maria the love of Christ, and the Lord softened her heart. She accepted Him as her Savior, but later she died of the leukemia.

The Enemy's Involvement

Let me ask you. Is it normal for a two- or three-year-old to be so emotionally hardened that the adults around her are amazed? There's no way. Human factors may be involved—an absent, uncaring mother, for instance—yet we cannot explain Maria's condition in merely human terms. The demonic influence present in that house of prostitution could have easily been transferred to this girl.

Obviously, this was not a true adoption, but it still illustrates the principle of family iniquity. I'm saying that in cases where there is a problem, we need to consider the possibility that Satan may have gained ground in a child's life through the iniquities of the parents. If so, we need to stand against the enemy and take back that ground, or things will just get worse in the next generation.

This feels like a good place to stop and emphasize once again, we don't have to fear the enemy! He is a defeated foe. "Greater is he that is in you than he that is in the world" (1 John 4:4). I can't say this enough. Even children need not fear the enemy (see chapter 11).

I've alluded to this earlier, but one of the perceptions I battle in my ministry is the idea that those of us who do warfare counseling are obsessed with the enemy. That's simply not true. My passion and goal is to exalt the Lord Jesus Christ. We never want to give the enemy any undue credit or attention, or instill fear of him in the minds of God's people.

So although I deal with people who are struggling mightily in the area of enemy involvement, I'm not obsessed with this stuff. When I go home at night, I don't check behind the door or look under the couch before I sit on it. If a book falls on the floor, I don't stand against it in the name of Christ.

What God's Word Teaches

But when the Bible warns repeatedly that the effects of sin can be felt for generations in a family, we need to understand what God is telling us. So as you consider how your family can resist Satan's

HIGHER GROUND:
Family Iniquities and Curses

Family iniquities, or self-will in a particular area of life, can be passed from generation to generation. How do we stop the cycle and find freedom in Christ? Here are four basic action steps, which are discussed in greater detail later in the chapter.

1. Acknowledge the specific iniquity. For help in how to pray, read Daniel's prayer in Daniel 9:3-19.

2. Ask God to cleanse the iniquity in the blood of the Lord Jesus Christ.

3. Ask God to reclaim any ground given to Satan and tear down every stronghold.

4. Claim Psalm 103:17 that from now on, the righteousness of your family will be your heritage for your children and for future generations. Also, commit this great verse to memory.

For the breaking of a curse, here is a suggested prayer you may find helpful:

> Father, in the name of Jesus Christ, I come to you desiring to be free from all curses and their results. I thank you for saving me and cleansing me of my sin. I confess that I belong to you.
> I now confess and repent of all my sins, known and unknown. I now confess the sins of my forefathers. In the name of the blood of Jesus Christ I break and renounce the power of every demonic curse that was passed down to me by the sins and actions of others. I now renounce, break, and loose myself and my family from all demonic subjection to any human being who has in the past or is now controlling me or my family in any way contrary to the Word and the will of God. In the name of Jesus Christ, I break the power and hold of every curse that has come to me through disobedience—mine or my forefathers'. I claim release and freedom through the blood of Christ. Amen.

attacks, you must be alert to potential ancestral problems. Let's consider the teaching of the Scriptures on this important point.

The Old Testament

The first occurrence of this concept is in Exodus 20:5, in the giving of the Ten Commandments. After forbidding Israel to make or bow down to any "graven image," God tells Moses, "I the Lord thy God am a jealous God, visiting the iniquity of the fathers upon the children unto the third and fourth generation of them that hate me."

If this were the only time God said this, it would be no less important. But the same warning occurs at least four more times in the books of Moses: Exodus 34:7; Leviticus 26:39–40; Numbers 14:18; and Deuteronomy 5:9. In addition, the prophets refer to the concept of iniquity's, or sin's consequences upon children in Isaiah 14:21 and Jeremiah 14:20.

The reference in Leviticus 26 is very interesting. God is warning the people of Israel that if they are unfaithful to Him, He will bring punishment on them and drive them from the land. But if the people confess their iniquities and the iniquities of their fathers (v. 40), He will remember His covenant promises to previous generations and restore them (v. 42).

In other words, the blessings of righteousness and faithfulness to God pass on through generations. Why should it seem strange that the consequences of sin and rebellion against Him would do the same in modern times?

The New Testament

In the New Testament, two primary words are translated "iniquity," and they are used just about equally. One word focuses on the aspect of iniquity which is unrighteousness or wickedness, and a different word expresses iniquity as lawlessness. This latter word can even be translated "lawlessness."

It's interesting that these two words are used interchangeably in Matthew 7:23 and Luke 13:27, which are parallel passages. They're actually compound words, but to form the compound Matthew uses the former word and Luke the latter. Both are translated "iniquity" in the KJV. In the NIV, both are translated as "evildoers."

Since sin is an expression of our self-will, it helps me to think of iniquity as the expression of sinful self-will in a particular area. The fact that God speaks of a father's iniquities passing on to his descendants doesn't negate the mother's influence. It does underscore the tremendous influence and responsibility God gives to fathers.

I believe strongly that God has assigned the primary authority in the home to the father. It has to do with the protection I talked about earlier. Just as the church offers spiritual protection to believers, so the father gives spiritual protection to the home. If he is out of it spiritually, the protection is removed and the family is vulnerable.

Freedom from Family Iniquity

My counseling experience with family iniquities bears this out again and again. A father who is bound in iniquity can pass along a spirit of iniquity and open up his wife and children to the temptation and attacks of the enemy. And the results will be worse with each succeeding generation until the enemy's strongholds are torn down. I know one missionary to Irian Jaya who told how in his village children come out of the womb demon-possessed.[2]

Along with the steps to freedom I've already outlined, I take my counselees who are dealing with this issue through four simple steps to break the cycle of family iniquity:

1. Acknowledge the iniquity. We have a very clear biblical precedent for this act of confession. Nehemiah confessed the sins of his "father's house" in Nehemiah 1:6, and in 9:2 the whole "seed of Israel" confessed "the iniquities of their fathers." Daniel made the same confession in Daniel 9:16. In fact, I urge you to read all of his marvelous prayer (vv. 3-19).
2. Ask God to cleanse the iniquity in the blood of the Lord Jesus Christ. The blood of Christ is the cleansing agent of every sin (1 John 1:9), and it is the blood that can set you free from family iniquity.
3. Ask God to reclaim any ground given to Satan and tear down every stronghold. I encourage those I counsel to make this declaration: "In the name of Christ, I declare every legal hold and every legal ground of the enemy broken and destroyed. Satan has no legal right to harass my family. Thank you, Jesus, for setting me free."
4. Claim Psalm 103:17 that from now on, the righteousness of your family will be your heritage for your children and for future generations. Also, commit this great verse to memory.

Blessings and Cursings

The issue of curses being part of spiritual warfare may cause you to struggle as I once did. It's difficult to accept the idea that a curse can have any impact for the same reasons you and I have a hard time accepting the idea of demonic transfer or ancestral spirits. It's so non-Western. It doesn't fit our conservative theology. I said to myself more than once about ancestral curses: This was something that only happened in Bible times, and today it only happens "over there" in "heathen" lands.

But after some of my travels and encounters with people I decided I needed to do a thorough study of what God's Word says about curses. So I studied every passage in the Bible that dealt with curses. The first thing I saw was that the Bible usually links curses with blessings.

What do we typically do, however? We separate them. We say, "I'll take the blessings, but I don't want to hear about the curses."

What God's Word Says

But the Bible isn't a cafeteria line. We can't just choose the items we want to believe. The children of Israel enjoyed God's blessings for obedience. But if they disobeyed, they came under His curse. When Joshua read the law to the people, he read every word, including "the blessings and the cursings" (Joshua 8:34).

Another fact I soon learned about curses is how powerful they are. I read of a husband who told his father-in-law that if anyone had his household idols in their possession, he should let that person die (Genesis 31:32). Jacob pronounced that curse not knowing that his wife Rachel had stolen the idols, and she died in childbirth.

King Saul put a curse on anyone who ate food on a certain day (1 Samuel 14:24). Who ate food, not knowing about the curse? Saul's own son, Jonathan, who later died in battle.

But to me the most amazing account is that of King David after his adultery with Bathsheba. When the prophet Nathan came to David and told him the story about the rich man who stole the poor man's pet lamb, David became enraged and decreed that the one who had done this should pay back the debt "fourfold" (2 Samuel 12:5–6). This was really a curse on the guilty party.

Nathan then revealed that David was the guilty man, and we see how his own curse of fourfold payment fell upon his family. David himself did not die, but in the course of time he lost four sons: the baby conceived in the adultery (2 Samuel 12:19), Amnon (13:29), Absalom (18:14), and Adonijah (1 Kings 2:24-25).

Let me tell you, when you see this in Scripture you can't escape the fact that curses are legitimate. No wonder God says we are not to curse people, but to bless. If you want a good study in Scripture, check out the places where a family put its special blessing on a member.

When our daughter Cheryl got married, we wanted to do something more than just give her away. We wanted to make the occasion very special. I began reading the Scriptures and asking God what our family could do to send my daughter into her marriage with something special to cherish.

I remembered the story of Rebekah, when Abraham's servant came to her home in search of a bride for Isaac (Genesis 24). Rebekah's family sent her on her way to Isaac with a blessing (v. 60). As soon as I read that, I knew what we could do. So the last thing before we left for the church for the wedding was to gather at the front door of our house and pray a family blessing on Cheryl. It was a beautiful thing. When our son got married, we gathered at the church and my wife and I prayed for wisdom for him as he started a new family.

Family Curses

Families can put curses on their children. In the case of parents or other family members who are practicing occultists or Satan worshipers, the curse may be some form of ritual that prescribes harsh punishment for anyone who leaves the group or reveals its secrets. We're told that members of organized crime take an oath of loyalty and secrecy on pain of death for any violations.

But many other families who have never been involved in any of this still curse their children. Fathers can curse their children by withholding their blessing or by crippling the children emotionally through abuse or constant criticism. Tell a child often enough that he's worthless and will never amount to anything and it becomes a self-fulfilling prophecy. He will live up, or should I say down, to those expectations.

How many fathers do you know who have blessed their sons? How many sons would give anything for their fathers' blessing? Many nights when I was growing up, I wept for just a little bit of a blessing from my father. I didn't know anything about the Bible. All I wanted was some word of approval from my dad.

If a curse is something that opens a person up to the influence of the enemy, then I believe these kinds of things are curses in the truest sense of the word. The reason is they have the same effect as a curse. If the person believes the lie contained in the curse—"you're no good," for example—the enemy has gained a foothold in his life from which he can build strongholds built on more lies.

I've mentioned how the deep sense of worthlessness and inferiority I inherited from my upbringing had tremendous repercussions in my life long after I became a Christian. Not only was I terrified almost to the point of paralysis by a fear of rejection and what people would think of me, I also remember other effects. I thought, for instance, that I had to have perfect kids or people would reject me and not like us. Imagine the pressure that put on my kids. The children would say, "Who cares what people think?" Their dad cared, because I was afraid.

I had to have a new car to feel better about myself. But long after the new-car smell went away, the payments didn't. This stronghold touched every area of my life. But when the truth came, it crumbled like the walls of Jericho.

Breaking the Curse

If there is evidence that a person in counseling is suffering from the effects of a curse, I try to deal with that as a separate issue. Since many of the people who come to me have a history of occultic or satanic involvement, it's very possible that they may have taken some sort of oath or even pledged themselves to Satan and put themselves under a curse.

As in all of our counseling and praying, there is nothing magic about the words. The power is in the person and name of Christ. The "Higher Ground" section on page 112 includes a suggested prayer for breaking this particular stronghold of the enemy.

Though the thought of curses is sobering and at times frightening, God gives us great encouragement in the Scriptures. We end this chapter with a great spiritual truth about our deliverer, Jesus Christ. As the apostle Paul noted in Galatians 3:10–14, Christ broke the greatest curse of all, "the curse of the law" that the entire human race was under because of our sin and failure to live up to God's perfect law. We can rejoice today that Jesus became a curse for us so that we could enjoy the blessings of salvation!

— 9 —
A FATHER AND HUSBAND'S PROTECTION

Spiritual warfare involves men and women on many different levels, but Satan's battle plan includes a special emphasis on adults in their vital roles as parents and spouses. Satan knows that if he can undermine the leaders of families, he undercuts God's plans to demonstrate His love in the special institution that He created, marriage. Therefore, if you're a husband, a father, a wife, or a mother, this chapter (and the next) are crucial to understanding how you are attacked and how to respond to satanic influences.

Helping Father Know Best

Fathers and husbands have a tremendous responsibility for their families—greater than anything I suspected when I got married. When I said "I do," I didn't realize all I had to do! We'll deal with the man as a husband a little later on. For now, we need to talk about a father's incredibly important role in spiritual warfare.

As a father, I really did not start getting it together spiritually until I was pastoring my second church in Tacoma, Washington. As I've said before, my wife is a very godly woman. She was doing a super job with our children—maybe too good of a job, because I didn't feel like I had to do anything. *Marguerite is doing such a great job, what can I add?* I told myself.

A Father's Responsibility

But the more I studied Scripture, the more I realized how much the Scriptures say about the responsibilities of fathers. One thing that bothered me was the reference in the Ten Commandments to the "iniquity of the fathers" (Exodus 20:5). We talked about this some in chapter 8, but I want to consider this truth again in light of the father's role.

This word *iniquity* occurs many times in the Old Testament. (I encourage you to trace the word's use yourself.) A friend of mine who used to teach Hebrew at a Bible college agreed to do some quick homework on the meaning of this word in the original language. He came back with a five-dollar definition, so I asked what it would mean in simple terms. "Put it into Logan," I asked him. We talked for a few minutes and I finally asked him, "Are you saying that iniquity is self-will?"

"Jim," he answered, "that's a good definition." Iniquity is self-will in a particular area, which fits so well with what we have been saying about the spiritual life. That is, any area of your life you don't want the Holy Spirit to control, Satan will seek to control.

A Father's Influence

If Exodus 20:5 and other verses like it teach anything, they teach that whatever iniquity plagues a father can affect his family for generations. The very area where a dad is in bondage will be the thing Satan uses to trip up his kids.

In my family the iniquity was alcoholism. Not only my father, but so many in the family were heavy drinkers. I grew up with beer and liquor in the house and thought every family was like mine. It seemed normal to me. As a child, I was allowed to have a little glass of beer from time to time. Not a full glass, not enough to get drunk on, but enough to develop a taste for beer.

This is a major reason I don't drink today. I feel it's not right for me as a Christian, but I also have to be careful because I know my family has been plagued with this problem for generations, and I don't want to open myself up to bondage in this area.

For many of the families I counsel, the bondage is sexual in nature. So often we try to work with a teenager, only to discover that his father is in bondage. Dad is experiencing some defeat, but his son is suffering terrible sexual defeat. There has to be a correlation.

That's why when a dad calls me with a child who's having a problem, the first thing I do is ask the dad permission to ask one question: "Are you experiencing victory in your personal moral life?"

Often the answer is no, which helps explain why even young children can be in sexual trouble. Some of the fathers who call me have heard me teach and know what I'm going to ask, so they brace themselves and almost grab the table as I ask their permission to inquire about their personal lives.

All of this reinforces a fact I believe is true: Any sin a father practices in moderation, his children will practice to excess.

A father's influence is so formidable that even if his children are too young or otherwise unable to imitate his actual sins, the children still come under great attack. Bill, our friend with the terrible sexual addiction, is once again a classic illustration. We've talked about the effects of his bondage on his wife, but what about his five children? As Bill admits,

> When I tried taking my life in a dark garage, I had no idea that I was allowing the evil one to bring the same destructive thoughts of death to my children. We now know that three of them had terrible thoughts of death following the "breach in the wall" (see Proverbs 25:28).
> . . . How [else] can I explain that our nine-year-old daughter was visualizing ways to mutilate, torture, and kill people, or that our eight-year-old daughter was considering different methods to take her own life? For months, we had had to discipline our three-and-a-half-year-old son for blatant disobedience.

I said there was a happy ending to this story. After Bill and his wife came to freedom, they stood against the evil spirits trying to destroy their children. God mightily answered their prayers for this family, and today Bill, his wife, and their six children (a new child has arrived) are still living in victory. One day I called Bill, and his ten-year-old daughter answered. I told her who I was and asked to speak to her dad.

"Oh, Mr. Logan, Mr. Logan!" she said. "I want to thank you for our family for setting my daddy free. Will you come to our house someday so we can meet you?" I just started crying. Bill's freedom had freed his family, and that remains one of the best thank-yous I've ever had.

A Father's Protection

Bill's experience underscores again that God put a father in the home to be the protector of that home, to shield his wife and children from destructive influences. What we as fathers allow to come into our homes will either have a positive or negative effect on our families. God wants a father to be very sensitive to this so that the atmosphere of his home is conducive to raising children who love Christ and desire to follow Him.

In our home, Marguerite and I were fairly strict with rules—not to be legalistic, but in a sincere desire to nurture our four kids in the things of Christ. They couldn't go a lot of places and do a lot of things other kids could. I asked them later, "Were we too strict?" Their answer was no, because they knew we loved them and wanted what was best for them. They didn't always agree with us, but they knew we acted out of love. That was very encouraging to me, and I hope it is to any parent who is reading this.

Even when parents make mistakes—and most of us make a lot of them—we will still do a good job if we will cover everything we do with love. Children are resilient, and they will forgive a lot and overlook a lot if they know they are loved. Kids need to be loved by their dads. They need to be touched appropriately by their dads.

If a father is so important to the spiritual life of his family, where do you think the enemy will attack to get a family off course? He'll attack the father. I think we have a hint of this in Jesus' description of a strong man under attack: "When a strong man armed keepeth his palace, his goods are in peace; but when a stronger [man] than he shall come upon him, and overcome him, he taketh from him all his armour wherein he trusted, and divideth his spoils" (Luke 11:21–22).

Jesus adds in Mark 3:27, "No man can enter into a strong man's house, and spoil his goods, except he will first bind the strong man." In order to spoil a home, Satan has to attack and bind the father, the "strong man," and then go after his family. The word *goods* here can even refer to the wife.

That's why, as I said above, when a family calls me with a child in trouble, I want to talk with the father first. I need to know what shape his spiritual life is in before we can deal with the child. When Dad is in defeat and even bondage, Satan has bound the strong man and is spoiling his house. If we're engaged in spiritual warfare, then the father is to be the warrior-protector of his family.

The issue we're talking about is authority, and another word for authority is *protection* (see the section on rebellion in chapter 5). As God's appointed authority in the home, a father who is walking in obedience to the Lord offers spiritual protection to his family.

Father Brings Benefits

The benefits that a godly father brings to his home are enormous. But the principle of spiritual protection does not mean that his children will be perfect or never stray from the path.

A child may willfully choose to remove himself from his father's protection and go into rebellion, but that's a different story. I've seen many cases like this too, so I don't want to give you the idea that every child in trouble has a father who's failing spiritually in some area.

I've had kids in my office with upside-down crosses carved in their skin, where they drew the blood as part of a satanic ritual. A young man who was a "skinhead" once came to see me. Shaved bald, angry, and intolerant of certain people, Greg was an imposing figure even as a teenager. I asked him why he was into this way of living.

"I like the feeling of power I have walking down the street with my friends," he responded honestly. "People will look at us, and they're afraid!"

This was a Christian young man, yet he was out beating people up. When Greg was in my office, though, the swagger was almost gone. He leaned forward and said, "But I'm tired of this. I'm sick of this life and want to change."

I praise God for the opportunity to work with Greg, but the point I want to make is that rebellion can get a terrible grip on a young person's life, even a young Christian's life.

How a Father Resists

In other words, nothing is "canned" or automatic in the Christian life. We know that from the teaching of Scripture and from experience. A father's spiritual protection does not exempt his family from Satan's attacks. We're still in a war with the enemy of our souls. But what an awesome difference a godly father makes when those attacks come. In the power of the Lord we fathers can resist Satan.

The Example of Job

Consider the example of Job; that's exactly what God asked Satan to do (Job 2:3) as He pointed to an example of how a godly father receives from his heavenly Father protection against Satan when he abides in Him. The only way the enemy could bring destructive attacks upon Job as a father was with God's permission. Satan said to God, "I can't touch him. He's your man. You've put a hedge around him" (see Job 1:10). Satan was right. Job was a righteous man, and God delighted in him.

Of course, that's just the beginning of the story. God gave Satan permission to bring terrible attacks on Job and his children. Everything fell apart in terms of order and stability in Job's life. Through Job's wife, Satan even tempted him to "curse God and die." What's going on here?

The first thing we need to understand is that God did not remove His hedge of protection from around Job. He allowed Satan to fire his flaming missiles at Job and his family, to be sure. And those missiles hit home with destructive force. But the early chapters of Job illustrate a crucial principle of spiritual warfare that we all need to grasp as believers: when the flaming missiles of Satan pass through God's hedge of protection, they cease to be Satan's destructive missiles and become instead the refining fire of God.

Job realized this. That's why, rather than curse God, Job *worshiped* Him (Job 1:20–22)! Isn't that amazing? Job didn't blame God for his calamities, and he didn't acknowledge Satan's involvement at all. What did Job say? "The Lord gave, and the Lord hath taken away; blessed be the name of the Lord" (v. 21).

Job knew that everything that happened to him was permitted by God for His purposes. When we are out of God's will, Satan doesn't need permission to attack us. But when we are walking in obedience and victory, we know that God has power and is protecting and refining us during the tough times. Satan can't lay a finger on us unless God allows it.

The Example of Peter

We have a perfect illustration of this in Luke 22, a chapter that's alive with demonic activity, by the way. Jesus told His disciple Peter that Satan wanted permission to sift him like wheat (v. 31). But Jesus was praying for Peter, that he would come through the temptation victoriously and be a tower of strength to the other disciples (v. 32).

Why did Jesus say this? Because Peter was about to fail miserably, denying the Lord three times. But God drew a line in Peter's life and said to Satan, "You can go this far, but no farther." Think about the difference between Peter and another disciple, Judas. The enemy had Judas so firmly in his grasp that Judas not only denied the Lord but destroyed himself.

Now I realize that God's larger purpose comes into play in Judas's case. His role was prophesied. But Peter sinned grievously, too, in his betrayal of the Messiah, and Peter's remorse was deep. Why didn't he give in to despair and take his life? After all, we know that self-destruction is Satan's ultimate plan for us.

Other than remorse, we're not told what thoughts Peter entertained after his sin. But we know that Jesus was praying for him, that the enemy would not gain the advantage in his life.

The Prayers of Jesus

As He did for Peter, Jesus is praying for us. That ought to be a tremendous encouragement to us fathers, and to every child of God. Today He is praying that we will stand strong. As long as we are walking in purity and obedience to the Lord, Satan still needs His permission to touch us. That's why I call Luke 22:31–32 a "Job statement" in the New Testament.

It's true that Peter failed and had to be restored. Similarly, Job still had some things to learn about God. That's what the remaining chapters of the book of Job are all about. But Peter became the fearless preacher at Pentecost, and God "blessed the latter end of Job more than his beginning" (Job 42:12).

Don't miss the point. There is a vast difference between the temptations that God allows to pass through His hedge of protection, and those that come because a father has opened up himself and his family to the enemy's influence by yielding to sin.

Dad, you have a great responsibility—but you also have great resources at your disposal. "Stand fast therefore in the liberty wherewith Christ hath made [you] free" (Galatians 5:1).

What about Husbands?

We've already said a lot about a man's role as husband, both directly and by implication. In the next chapter we will consider the ways that Satan can come against women and the resources they have to resist and stand firm. But before we make this turn, I have another extraordinary testimony of a father who accepted his responsibility as a husband as well. We fathers must remember that while godly actions protect our families, especially our children, we also are responsible as husbands to protect our wives. Someone has wisely said, "The best thing a father can do for his children is to love their mother."

Mike's action came after his failure and was designed to rebuild his marriage and restore his wife's trust. He had failed morally, and now he repented of his sin. But he also recognized that a spiritual battle (which he had been losing) was at the root of his fall. This led him to draw up a detailed battle plan under the guidance of the Holy Spirit in order to repair the breach in the walls of his home.

Maintaining Trust

His remarkable story shows God's forgiving and restoring grace in action. Husbands can and must maintain their wives' trust. Here is Mike's story, accompanied by the actual plan [see "A Husband's Battle Plan"] he drew up, a plan any man can use to express his love and to prevent a moral fall. (Mike has given us permission to include both his battle plan and his testimony.)

If Mike's name sounds familiar, you're right. We met "Dr. Mike" in chapter 5, as he resisted the idea he was vulnerable as a Christian. His sobbing confession years later of moral failure was the prelude to his finding release from satanic influence through pornography. Mike's story of bondage to pornography shows how a husband who has yielded ground to Satan also makes his wife and children vulnerable.

> I was introduced to pornography around the ages of 9–12 when I found my father's supply. Whenever he was gone, I would look at the pictures and read the stories. So-called friends also had pornography, usually at their homes. This led to other immoral episodes. This con-

HIGHER GROUND:
A Husband's Battle Plan

Below is the action plan Mike drew up and committed himself to follow after his moral failure. It's a terrific plan, whether a husband has failed his wife or not. In fact, this is a great way for a husband to put his love in action and set up barriers to temptation that could lead deep into sexual sin. We commend it to you—not as a temporary "fix," but as a workable, God-honoring daily discipline.

1. Make a vow to your wife that you will share any wrong thinking or action before you go to bed at night (Ephesians 4:26).

2. Affirm to your wife, "Now that God has delivered me from bondage, I will still be out from under bondage no matter what happens. Even if something were to happen to you, I will still be free because I now consider myself to be "dead unto sin, but alive unto God in Christ Jesus" (Romans 6:11, 17).

3. Purpose to read Scripture daily to your wife from now on (Ephesians 5:26).

4. Make time with your wife early in the day a daily priority.

5. Commit yourself to a consistent daily quiet time and to spiritual growth.

6. Tell your wife often, "I'm really free." Give her examples of the changes in your life.

7. Write your wife little notes regularly, telling her things like "I'm fine, and I love you." Make sure she understands what "I'm fine" means:
   a. The shield of faith is up to reject any wrong thoughts.
   b. You are obeying the Holy Spirit's promptings in thoughts and actions.
   c. You are not thinking wrong thoughts.
   d. You are holding to your vow to share any wrong thoughts or actions with her before bedtime.
   e. You are conscientiously looking away from wrong magazines, commercials, immodest dress, or other traps of Satan.
   f. You are daily renewing your relationship with Jesus.

8. Keep your relationships formal with other women to protect your marriage.

tinued until I was 21, when I gave my life to Christ. From then on there was no more pornography, but all that ground had been given to Satan and strongholds were built on that ground. Later, I didn't realize the pattern of satanic strongholds that had been built in my mind because I dealt with each failure as a single event and as scripturally as I knew how at the time.

During this time I was growing spiritually, though with isolated incidents of moral failure. Despite this dark side of my life, I got involved in a good church and met my future bride. We dealt with things in her life, but didn't recognize or deal with the root problems in my life. Following our marriage I thought things would change, but 10 years of struggle ensued. Satan was looking for an opportune moment.

Some years later I heard Jim Logan speak on spiritual warfare. I didn't understand it all, but I did think it related to us—I thought my wife was the problem! How deceived I was. And prideful! I heard a testimony on taking back ground and tearing down strongholds from a man with a moral failure problem, but in my pride I suppressed the problem and thought, "I've conquered that."

Some time later, we found ourselves with a new job, new baby, and new neighborhood, but no regular church home for input and accountability. I was getting more deeply involved than ever in moral sin, and even though I was doing a lot of right things spiritually I didn't understand all the ground I had given to Satan and the jurisdiction he still had in my life. Because of this, and my lack of alertness to Satan's schemes, I fell into major moral failure. After several weeks, I confessed to my wife—but it was a lukewarm, partial confession that only hurt and angered her more. I realized my major sin was against Jesus. I followed with a complete confession and saw that my only hope was deliverance from this bondage.

I called Rev. Logan to arrange counseling. During the 3 + months before I could go, my wife and I had a very difficult relationship. At Jim Logan's office, God not only delivered me from my moral failure, but showed me my problem with pride and bitterness. I asked God to forgive these sins, take back the ground, and tear down Satan's strongholds. Now I had a lot of rebuilding to do. These were difficult times because of how badly I had damaged my marriage. But I was able to stay pure because Satan had no more ground in my life and his strongholds were being torn down! When I released my wife from the need to "police" my behavior, a tremendous burden was lifted from her shoulders.

The "rebuilding" Mike referred to took time. He recognized that his marriage lacked the closeness of prior times, but he also felt God giving him "a heightened desire to please my wife." So he began some important rebuilding steps, described in "A Husband's Battle Plan." During the next eighteen months their relationship was strained and distant.

"It would have been much easier for us to give up, but our commitment to our covenant with God upheld us during these terrible days," Mike explained. "After almost a year of my following these rebuilding steps, my wife's heart began to change and her trust began to rebuild.

"The result was that I received an unexpected gift—my wife's heart was turned back to me! I took my wife through the same steps to freedom that Rev. Logan took me through. God delivered her from bitterness and rebellion. I am so grateful to God for my deliverance."

Mike has been delighted to find his wife refreshed and happy in their marriage. "The light is back in my wife's eyes and she is joyful again. By God's grace, I still walk in victory. My wife has a new love for me and increased reliance on God. And our physical relationship has never been closer. We live for Him."

There isn't anything I can add to that except to say, praise the Lord!

Granting Freedom

A second way we fathers can be spiritual leaders is to grant our wives freedom in directing the house. Too many of us husbands don't give our wives enough freedom to operate in their world. Generally speaking, a woman enjoys the special elements of having a home. There she builds memories and part of her identity; it's an important part of her world. Often, she will see things differently in her world than you will. Your view is neither better nor worse than hers, but it is different. You should respect her views and grant her freedom to largely establish the home's feel.

As a husband, be aware of different expectations you have, and acknowledge that you may not always have the right perspective. You need your wife's input. Again, sometimes your perspective is not right or wrong compared with your wife's; it's just a matter of preference. In those cases, we men need to yield at times, both out of love and the recognition that our way is not the only way.

A husband needs to be sensitive to his wife's concerns, desires, and ideas in her world. He needs to give his wife more room to move, and to make her world as safe, secure, and functional as possible. Men, we and our wives have important jobs to do in creating homes of godly influence. Let's do them together, as a team.

— 10 —
A WIFE AND
MOTHER'S LASTING BEAUTY

When we look at pictures of battle and warfare, we usually see men with dirt on their faces and torn battle jackets. When we watch scenes of warfare, we usually hear lots of male grunting. But the picture is incomplete when we're discussing spiritual warfare, for women are not exempt. Women are soldiers in the battle as well.

As wives and mothers, several warfare issues will confront you in particular. And, with the Lord on your side, you can have victory too. The following guidelines are based on material I've presented to many women's seminars and groups; I am grateful to my wife and to the many women who have given me good feedback and have helped me to sharpen my thinking on the spiritual struggles women face.

The Proper Focus

To understand where women are especially vulnerable to the enemy's attack, we need to see what the Scriptures indicate a woman's emphasis should be as a wife and mother. In 1 Peter 3:3, the apostle urges a woman not to place all her attention on her outer beauty. One obvious reason is that no matter how young and attractive a person may be today, time and gravity are against all of us! If we put all of our emphasis on physical beauty, it will lead to disappointment. Our flesh is corrupting.

Instead, Peter calls on a godly woman to develop two qualities of the spirit that will make her more and more beautiful as the years go by, because these things never corrupt. The two qualities that will make any woman extremely beautiful are found in verse 4, "the ornament of a meek and quiet spirit, which is in the sight of God of great price."

By looking at these inner attributes of meekness and quietness— and particularly their opposites—we can see the two areas where a woman is most vulnerable to Satan's influence, because they touch on what is deepest within her.

A Woman's Most Vulnerable Areas

Anger

Meekness as used here in 1 Peter 3 and elsewhere in the New Testament is a gentleness or serenity of spirit. For example, the New International Version translates *meekness* in Galatians 5:23 as *gentleness.* The opposite of meekness is anger.

Women get angry just as men do. It's part of what makes us human. But women tend to get angry in a different way than men do, and the kind of anger women are most prone to can make them vulnerable to attacks from the enemy.

Author and family counselor Gary Smalley observes that men tend to express anger physically, while women are more likely to express anger verbally.[1] A man's anger is often triggered by a specific event, which causes him to blow up.

A woman's anger, however, is very often born of frustration that builds over time. It may be her husband's indifference to a concern she expresses or a request she makes of him, or perhaps she may have an overall sense of frustration that things at home or at work are not going well, that others are not pulling their share of the load. Let me show you two types of anger as they're mentioned in Scripture. First, *thumos* can be characterized as "turbulent commotion, boiling indignation," anger that flares up and burns out quickly like a match that has been lit. This is a common word for anger that is used in Ephesians 4:31, Galatians 5:20, and other places.[2]

This describes the "Mount St. Helens" type of anger, the one men have the most. This is the kind of anger that blows up, and everybody is devastated by the fallout. The man explodes and everything is covered with three feet of ashes, but the pressure has been relieved. As men are prone to say, "There, I got it off my chest. I feel much better." Those around the man may not feel better, but at least he does. The volcano cools, and the man returns to normal (though typically the volcano is only dormant; it may erupt again some other day).

The other New Testament word for anger I want you to notice is *orge.* This is "a more settled and long lasting attitude often continuing toward the goal of seeking revenge." The verb form of this word, with an added Greek prefix, means to be provoked to irritation, exasperation, or embitterment.[3] The verb can be used in a positive sense, as in Ephesians 4:26. The noun form *orge* appears in Ephesians 4:31, where it is translated as *anger,* in Colossians 3:6, and in James 1:20 among many other places.

This word is also used to describe the burning of charcoal. You know how charcoal burns. It's hard to start, but once it's truly fired up, it stays real hot long after the meat is done. This is the slow burn, the seething kind of anger that women are especially vulnerable to and must guard against.

I have seen this settled kind of anger in the lives of a number of women, often in the wives of the men I counsel. That should not be surprising, because these men usually have real problems that in many cases drive their wives to distraction in addition to the damage it does in their own lives.

Judy was very angry with her husband. It was an accumulation of many things over the years, mostly frustration at what her husband was not doing to take his place as leader in the home and be the protector and encourager she wanted him to be. By the time I talked to her, Judy's anger had turned into bitterness—and she got mad at me for suggesting that her bitter attitude had become part of the problem rather than something she was entitled to.

Counselors like Gary Smalley and many others who work with great numbers of people recognize that women are generally more emotionally "tuned in" and sensitive than men.[4] That's a wonderful quality that any man in his right mind would cherish in a woman, but it also leaves women vulnerable to slow, burning anger—and the attacks of the enemy.

Satan would love nothing better than to exploit a woman's frustration with her husband and push her toward the devastating emotion of bitterness. Then she begins to attack and tear down her husband rather than show him respect, and he will react to her anger. Now the enemy has both spouses bound up, and the children are wide open for harassment. Anger is such a powerful emotion that the only safe way to handle it is to follow Paul's admonition in Ephesians 4:26. Deal with it quickly, do not let a day pass where it can build and harden into bitterness.

Fear

The second quality Peter commends to godly women is a "quiet spirit." This does not mean simply choosing not to talk. The idea is a heart that trusts in God and rests in Him. So the opposite of a quiet spirit is a fearful spirit, not a talkative one. It has nothing to do with how much you say, but everything to do with a calm, trusting attitude that dispels fear. Every woman can have such a spirit.

As a woman, are you allowed to fear? Yes, according to Scripture, you can have one fear, a holy fear—the fear or reverence for God. In fact, Peter mentions this in verse 2, when he calls on wives to display a chaste behavior toward their husbands, "coupled with fear."

The kind of fear I'm talking about is in verse 6. Again, I like the way the NIV translates the last phrase of the verse: "do not give way to fear." This could also be translated, "Don't give in to hysterical fear." When a woman does that she tends to take things in her own hands—things she wasn't supposed to take on.

Women struggle with a fearful spirit. That's why they get angry sometimes, and that's why they need that quiet trust in God. A woman sees so much more than a man sees. She walks into the house, sees a crack in the wall, and knows something ought to be done. Her husband, however, waits until the roof is blown off and the water is pouring in. Then he says wisely, "You know, honey, we ought to do something about this." His wife is thinking, "Thank goodness. I've been praying you'd do something about this for twenty years!"

Clearly, a woman's concerns often are justified. Many women have a unique sense of danger and even of a person's goodness or threat. What we call women's intuition is really a woman's heightened ability to discern situations. So it's OK to have concern.

The problems come when those concerns degenerate into fear and anxiety. When fear takes over, we are denying God's ability to control the situation and His desire to look after our welfare. If a woman is trusting in her husband to take care of everything, she is certain to have times of fear. Is it because husbands are not dependable? Not necessarily. It's that women are to put their trust in God, not in their husbands (see 1 Peter 3:5). Women are to respect their husbands, but they are never told to trust their husbands—not in the way they are to trust God. This is a vitally important distinction.

Among the fears many mothers have is how they are rearing their children. They wonder how they should discipline them, educate them, spend leisure time with them. Joyce, in her late twenties, was afraid to discipline her five-year-old son. It seems she had read some articles about child abuse, and was terrified that if she corrected Jonathan with physical discipline, she would abuse him. This fear paralyzed Joyce. When I talked with her, I saw none of the symptoms or signs that indicated she would be an abusive parent. Her love was genuine and her self control was obvious. In the meantime, her son was cruising along getting his own way all the time.

I believe the enemy had bound Joyce in irrational fear and was using his intruding thoughts to keep her from exercising her proper role. I discussed with her some of the principles we've been studying in this book, and she seemed to come to a greater peace about the situation.

Another important area where a woman can become angry or fearful is when her concerns or desires for her children are not shared by her husband. A couple of examples will help illustrate what I mean.

Let's assume for a moment a fairly typical family—dad, mom, and a teenager. The teenager, Wayne, is starting to use what our grandparents called "sass" or "back talk." This needs to be dealt with, or it can easily lead to open rebellion against authority and eventual disaster.

In this typical home, the mother is the main target of her sassy teenager, both because mom is around a lot more and because Wayne knows what would happen if he talked to his dad like that.

Mom is very concerned about her son, because women have a wonderful ability to look ahead and see how a particular behavior will affect their children long-term. She knows that if Wayne doesn't learn to obey an authority he can see—i.e., his parents—he won't be ready to obey an authority he can't see—God.

So this mother says to her husband, "You need to talk to your son." But dad's processes are working differently. First, he doesn't want a confrontation that forces him to talk about stuff like emotions and behavior. Second, because men tend to look at things like this in a much more sweeping and less carefully defined sense than a woman, dad figures that as long as Wayne hasn't run afoul of the law, been tossed out of school, or had some other crisis that would cause dad to be bothered, everything is fine. So he basically ignores his wife's plea for help in disciplining Wayne.

I've presented this with a bit of a light touch, but there's nothing funny about the fear and/or anger a woman can feel when, deep down, she realizes her husband doesn't share her concerns. A woman caught in the middle like this needs to appeal to her husband as the authority in the home. If he doesn't respond, then his wife has to do the hard thing: release him to the Lord and trust God to bring the right pressure to bear at the right time rather than verbally attacking her husband.

Though it speaks of kings, Proverbs 21:1 contains a great reminder about husbands: "The king's heart is in the hand of the Lord, as the rivers of water: he turneth it whithersoever he will." There are two things that change the course of a river: time and pressure. A man tends to push away from him any person who puts pressure on him—including his wife. As a wife, if you relent, releasing your husband to the Lord, He can change your husband's heart because your husband is responding to the right pressure—pressure from God and not from his wife.

In other cases, there may be a legitimate difference of expectations on the part of your husband and you—whether it's concerning the

HIGHER GROUND:
A Wife's Battle Plan

Like the battle plan for men in chapter 9, the following steps are excellent suggestions for any woman who wants to strengthen her walk with Christ. They are the steps Mary (see chapter 1) took to find peace and true freedom in the Lord when her husband was cold and rejecting toward her before he came to freedom in Christ.

1. Seek to have your needs for love, comfort, and companionship fulfilled in Christ. He will meet you in your need.

2. Tell the Lord that although you want to see your husband change, to find freedom in Christ, or whatever your desire is, it is all right with you if this doesn't happen, because Christ is enough. If you cannot say this, ask the Lord to make you willing.

3. Pray that God will bring about your husband's deliverance in His time and way (Psalm 46:10).

4. Pray that God will make you the wife you need to be, and that He will love your husband through you.

5. Present your body to God as a living sacrifice to use as He wills (Romans 12:1–2).

6. Ask God to make real in your life the truth of 2 Corinthians 5:15: "He died for all, that they which live should not henceforth live unto themselves, but unto him which died for them, and rose again." Choose to see yourself as dead in Christ, and you'll feel more alive than ever.

7. Occasionally in your prayer life, lay aside your requests and supplications and focus on God's greatness, power, and love. Read a hymn aloud to the Lord.

8. Seek not just an outward response of love toward your husband, but a heart of love to help you avoid the bitterness that can develop and open you up to demonic attack.

children's future, work, how the finances should be handled, or a hundred other things. These are times when a husband and wife can help each other see a different side of the issue and sharpen each other's outlook. Of course, a wife may also come to the place where her husband insists on a certain course of action. When that happens, a wife needs to put her trust in the Lord, rest in Him, and release her husband and the issue to God.

Dealing with Areas of Vulnerability

When things don't happen like they should and plans don't unfold as they ought, it's easy for you as a woman to become angry and fearful. What spiritual resources can you draw on to protect yourself in these areas of vulnerability?

The Proper Trust

One resource every woman has is mentioned in 1 Peter 3:5, where the apostle calls it a mark of a godly woman: *trust.* The holy women of old "trusted in God." As I said above, God never asks a woman to trust her husband. Husbands are not trustworthy. If you put your trust in a person, any person, what will happen eventually? You'll be let down.

Most women have a strong mothering instinct, which many insincere men try to appeal to in order to flatter women. If two people like this—a woman with a strong mothering instinct and a man who likes to feel mothered—get married, the woman will mother her husband. The numbers of such couples are legion. These relationships are doomed, because a woman isn't designed to lead her husband. He may like it initially, but before long the husband will resent her mothering. He may even say to her, "You're just like your mother."

"Yes, but you liked it before we got married," she will reply.

Many women try to protect their husbands from life's consequences, but if they do that they may be just prolonging his immaturity. I would point you back again to the testimony of Mary in chapter 1 of the book. In a very remarkable way, Mary released her husband to God, to let God deal with him. That's what a wife has to do.

Trust means you believe God has the power and desire to work out things the right way and that His call to submission on your part is wise. Remember, you are not trusting in your husband's actions or innate wisdom, but in God's ability to work things to His glory and good through your family situation.

The Proper Submission

A woman who tries too hard to protect her husband or her children can easily become fearful. But we know that God has not given us a spirit of fear (2 Timothy 1:7). I may not get a lot of "amens" on this one, but I think a second antidote to anger and fear, and a second mark of a godly woman, is *proper submission to her husband* (1 Peter 3:5–6). The husband and father is responsible to lead. Help him if necessary, but let him lead. "Be careful [or, "anxious"] for nothing" (Philippians 4:6) is a good word to wives here.

I believe anxiety is to the spirit what pain is to the body. If you try to lift a car to fix a flat tire, what will you feel in your back? Pain. Pain is good, because it tells me I am trying to lift a load that's too heavy for me.

"Do not be full of cares about any situation," Paul says. "Don't be anxious." When you feel anxious, respond properly. Anxiety is a call to prayer. We may not be able to avoid feeling anxious, but it's wrong to stay anxious. Anxiety never solved anything. What has worry ever done for you except make you sick?

The Proper Ornament

I don't want to overlook the first thing we talked about, "the ornament of a meek and quiet spirit" (v. 4). This is a tremendous protection against the anger and anxiety that can overtake a woman—and therefore, a tremendous protection against the harassment of the enemy. It's also, by the way, the third mark of a godly woman that Peter shares in this passage (v. 5a).

The ornament of a spirit that manifests gentleness and assurance in God is appealing to men. Demonstrate to your husband and your children such a spirit, and you become a model of how every member of the family can deal with anxiety. And, of course, you find that peace you need to defuse the anger or anxiety in your life.

The "Fiery Trial"

When it comes to spiritual warfare, as a woman you can expect temptation in one other area: crises of all sizes. Peter calls them "fiery trials," and they will surely come your way. In fact, the apostle tells us we can expect them (1 Peter 4:12).

That doesn't mean it's pleasant, however. What can be so painful for a woman about a fiery trial is that sometimes it can come from a source she doesn't expect—her husband.

When this happens, a woman has to be careful. She can go through her fiery trial either radiating with the glow of God or becoming bitter. Mary is a great example of a woman who refused to be consumed with bitterness against her husband, or even against God, and to open herself up to demonic attack.

As believers, we come under attack not in the spirit, for Christ resides there, but in the soul—in our minds, emotions, and wills. Satan can put thoughts in our minds and cause us to feel things that are not true.

Psychologists and other researchers who study male and female behavior conclude that men respond to situations typically with their minds: thinking, analyzing, and trying to move to a point of action; in contrast, women respond emotionally, concerned with relationships among people.

In my own counseling I have found the difference exists in spiritual warfare too. The result is women are very susceptible to being attacked in their emotions. Therefore, when you as a woman go through suffering that God allows to refine you, remember the need to guard your soul (1 Peter 4:19), because that's where Satan will attack. (Men must also be aware of satanic attacks, of course. But it will take a different form than assailing the emotions.)

Paul gives us one example of a woman's emotional vulnerability in 2 Corinthians 11:3, where he reminds us that the serpent "beguiled" Eve. That is, Eve became strongly convinced in her emotions of the truth of something that was in reality a lie. This is a very real possibility for a woman, and another area in which she needs to be on her guard.

A Mother's Influence

We can't leave this subject without taking a more focused look at the crucial role a mother plays in the life of her family. Allow me to share a few key thoughts with you here.

Time with the Children

One obvious reason a mother is so influential is that generally she is in the home and therefore with the children far more than her husband. So children are very likely to pick up on their mother's attitude toward them, toward their father, toward life in general, and toward God.

I often remind mothers that they can display every element of the fruit of the Spirit (Galatians 5:22–23) to their children as they (the moms) allow Christ to live His life through them. We now know that mothers can even affect their children before they are born. I know many expectant mothers who read the Word to their unborn children and sing to them.

The First Five Years

There's no way to get around the importance of a mother's influence on her children in the first five years of their lives. Young children need the kind of individual attention they can't get in a group setting. Someone has said that if children were meant to be raised in herds, then mothers would have litters!

I believe a mom's most important responsibility during these formative years is to teach her children the meaning of the word *no.* Now, you may be thinking, *Is he kidding? That's it?* Let me explain.

If a child is going to learn to obey God, he must learn to yield his will to the will of another. Guess who's the first significant "other" a child encounters? His mom, usually. She's the one who, more than anyone else begins and—we hope—completes the all-important job of teaching her children to respond properly to authority. This is so important that once a mother has accomplished this, the task of child-rearing is downhill from there.

Three Vital Qualities

As a mother, you can help your children develop habits and attitudes that will aid them in resisting satanic influence later in life. Three major character qualities a mom can focus on with her children are obedience to authority, responsibility, and gratitude. I sometimes ask mothers, "If you knew you would be removed from your daughter's life when she becomes twelve years old, what are the qualities you would most desire for her to have to prepare her for successful adulthood?" Many suggest one or more of these three qualities, and they are right.

By demonstrating obedience, responsibility, and gratitude before her children, a mother can help to instill those qualities in her kids. How do you handle annoyances or disappointments from neighbors, other parents, church members? Remember, your children are taking clues for their behavior and understanding of right and wrong from your behavior. A key way you can model obedience and gratitude is by how you respect and respond to your husband.

The influence a mother wields in her home is incredible. Proverbs 14:1 is a good verse for moms: "Every wise woman buildeth her house: but the foolish plucketh it down with her hands." The enemy used Job's calamities to get to his wife, who urged Job to curse God (Job 2:9). Job had to remind her that she was speaking like a foolish person (v. 10). In other words, he was saying to her, "Don't you realize you'll be tearing down your own house if I take your advice and curse God?"

As I said before, my wife, Marguerite, has been a terrific mother. Her crowning glory came when our three daughters said they wanted to be like her. Today she has the joy and privilege of being an intercessor for our six grandchildren, and our daughters still call her for advice on how to handle various things. This is the beauty of a lifelong relationship between a mother and her children, where love and commitment and trust have built a godly legacy. As the husband and father of this crew, I feel blessed just to be a part of it!

As a team, you and your husband have a great impact on your children. Working together can help you in protecting the family from evil influences while creating a home where godly influence abounds.

— 11 —
CHILDREN CAN RESIST TOO

Children may be innocent, but they are not immune from spiritual battle. Satan is a cruel enemy who does not spare the young. In fact, some of the most dramatic warfare experiences I've had, and some of the best lessons I've learned, have been with children. I don't think anyone would argue that children are immune to Satan's temptations and attacks. He does attack children, mainly when their parents are giving ground.

Childlike Faith

But even children under attack from the enemy don't have to be afraid. In fact, I find that children are generally much more believing and trusting in standing against Satan than a lot of adults. It is their childlike faith in Jesus and the Bible. Remember, Jesus commended a child's faith to the adults around Him as being the type that gained entry into heaven (Matthew 18:2–4; Mark 10:13–16).

Children also bring to life, and especially to spiritual things, a unique perspective and openness that sometimes makes for hilarious moments, reminding us that the Christian life is really not all that complicated.

Childlike Humor

Before we get into the subject of children and spiritual warfare, let's see how simple and yet profound children can be about spiritual things.

A mom I know listened one morning as she sat at the kitchen table between her two sons, who were deciding which one would pray.

"Benjamin, will you pray for us, please?" asked Zachary, age four.

"No," answered two-year-old Benjamin. (Benjamin doesn't know too many words.)

"Now Benjamin, if you have the Word of God in your hand, the Word of God says you should pray, and if you're ever in danger you should get on your knees and ask God to protect you because He is your shield, Benjamin."

"Mommy," Zachary asked, turning to his mother, "is my shield really the Lord Jesus Christ?"

"When a person is trusting the Lord Jesus to be their shield," Mom answered, "then He is their protector and shield."

"Well, Benjamin doesn't know the Lord, and he says yes to the fiery darts."

"Then you need to pray for Benjamin."

"Dear Jesus, please help Benjamin come to know the Lord so he will stop saying yes to the fiery darts."

With a prayer warrior like that for an older brother, I think Benjamin is going to be in good shape!

The Children's Mighty Defender

Children and spiritual warfare is another subject on which I could spend several chapters. For our purposes here, let's look at two important passages of Scripture relating to children. Both texts are familiar to you, I'm sure, but when you look at them in light of the principles of spiritual warfare, they come alive.

Both passages are in Matthew, 18:1–10 and 19:13–15. In both settings, Jesus has children at His side and commends them, holding up their faith as an example to the watching adults. Our tendency as adults is to sentimentalize these stories, treating them as touching little accounts of Jesus' love for children.

But Matthew 18:6–7 in particular contains some of the strongest language Jesus used anywhere. Many Bible teachers believe He referred to children's guardian angels in verse 10. And in 19:15, He put His hands on the children in blessing.

If Jesus is this strong in His protection and blessing of children, do you think He will come to their defense when the enemy attacks them? What would you do if you saw someone attacking your child in your own front yard? Jesus views those children who follow Him as important members of His kingdom, and He will protect them. Children have a mighty Defender to aid them in spiritual warfare.

Ways Children Can Be Vulnerable

If children are not immune to spiritual conflict and are often targets of Satan and his forces, then we need to deal with some important issues concerning children and spiritual warfare.

The first thing we need to understand is how children can come under the enemy's influence. I want to emphasize the word *influence* here because it's important to remember that Satan and evil spirits are spirits of influence. As suggested above, our children are not helpless prey for the enemy. Keep that in mind as we move through this section.

The Occult

One very obvious way children and young people can open them selves up to demonic influence is through occult activities such as Ouija boards, fantasy role-playing games, and many of the video games found at public arcades and available for home use. We discussed this is some detail in chapter 3.

Parents can't follow their children around for eighteen years, monitoring their every move. God never asked us to do that anyway. But I'm always amazed by how few Christian parents know, for example, what their children are watching on television—much less regulating their viewing. This is a great place to start.

You as a parent can take authority in your home and make sure you are not unwittingly allowing your children to expose themselves to evil by the video games they play. They may not even purchase the games and still could have access to inapropriate ones. Some kids borrow games from their friends or simply wait to hit the local mall or movie theater to play the arcade version.

Entertainment

My counseling experiences show this whole area of media and entertainment to be one of Satan's primary tools—and of course, I'm not the first person to notice that. You can spare your children and yourself a lot of problems by becoming very involved, informed, and aware of what's going on in this area. Be aware of the latest TV shows and video movies. And if your children play video games or listen to the radio (or visit friends who do), be aware of video games and music.

This also becomes a challenge to us as parents, because we have to make sure that we ourselves are not bringing evil influences into our homes via cable TV, reading material, or whatever. Remember, what you may simply "taste" occasionally, your children may devour! Why even take the risk?

Childish Fears

Another way children may come under the enemy's influence is when he exploits their natural, childish fears of things like a dark room, or the fear of separation. Many adults chuckle as they recall the feeling they had as children that something was under the bed, which made them afraid to dangle an arm or leg over the edge of the bed.

It may seem silly now, but it's a fear children often have, and it's not abnormal. Parents can help their children here by praying with them at night, reminding them of God's strong and comforting presence, and praying over them as they sleep.

This is another place where Christian parents can do a lot more than they think they can to protect their children. Television programs can leave children with terrible mental images of evil and danger. So we're back to the need to monitor the influences in our homes and to provide spiritually healthy, encouraging alternatives to the typical media fare the entertainment industry offers our children.

Another instance is Halloween. The controversy over whether to celebrate Halloween will always be with us. But when you view it from the perspective of spiritual warfare the question becomes, why should I as a parent seeking to guard my family from evil influences expose them needlessly to evil images and legends? Certainly we do not want our children celebrating with costumes that glorify evil or depict violent characters.

I do not pretend to have all the answers. It just seems to me that wise parents will take every opportunity to expose their children to the things of Christ and shield them from the ways and work of the enemy. He's seeking a foothold in their lives already. Why help him?

What the Scriptures Say

As I study the Scriptures, I see several passages that indicate ways in which children are vulnerable and what we can do to protect them. Let me show you what I mean.

Children are vulnerable first because they are very spiritually sensitive and trusting. The passages we looked at above in Matthew 18 and 19 indicate this, and also show us the importance of leading our children to Jesus rather than putting stumbling blocks in their path.

Children are also vulnerable because they are emotionally immature and therefore subject to being frustrated and discouraged by inconsistent or harsh parenting (Ephesians 6:4; Colossians 3:21). The remedy is to nurture them in the Lord, to know their particular "bent" (their tendency or predisposition, the idea behind the oft-quoted Proverbs 22:6), and deal with them accordingly.

Finally, children are vulnerable because they inherit the effects of the generations that preceded them—both for good and evil. This is the other side of the picture given in Exodus 20:5–6. If fathers can pass on both blessings and iniquities to their children, it follows that children receive an awful lot of things they have no control over.

Two Special Young Men

Joseph

The power of Christ to engage and overcome the enemy in spiritual warfare is never demonstrated more vividly than in the lives of children whose faith is growing and vital. With that in mind, let me introduce you to Joseph. I first met Joseph at a series of meetings I was holding with a particular mission; I was still in missionary work myself, serving with the mission as a vice-president and a counselor for the missionaries.

The missionaries' children, including Joseph, joined their parents for a meeting this particular night. I mentioned an experience I had just had back home. Because the story is integral to what happened subsequently with Joseph, let me briefly share it with you.

While driving to another conference, I turned on a network radio station in St. Louis. To my shock, a man was telling how to channel spirits. At first I didn't realize what was going on. But it soon became clear that this channeler had called up his spirit, supposedly someone who had lived in England one hundred years ago. The host was actually interviewing this spirit—and once you've heard a demon speak, it's easy to recognize.

So I listened, and at the end of the program this spirit said, "Are you lonely? Do you find yourself with no friends? There are a lot of us spirits out here waiting, and if you will right now invite us to come in, we will never leave you. We will never forsake you. We will be your friend. We will talk with you."

It was one of the most alluring invitations I ever heard! I just kept praying, "Lord, don't let an old person hear this. Don't let a lonely person hear this." It sounded so reasonable, so friendly.

I recounted the radio conversation to this audience of missionary parents and kids. As I shared this experience, little Joseph, who was about seven-and-a-half, heard a voice saying to him, "If you ask me in, I'll come in."

Obviously, I didn't know what was happening at the time. I noticed Joseph turning to his father and saying something, and then his dad took him off into the dark. We always took our kids out and "tuned them up" if they were distracting, so I just figured Joseph was getting "tuned up" out there somewhere. He and his dad never came back to the meeting.

What Joseph had done was tell his father about the battle going on inside of him. His father understood, because he had been a missionary in Alaska working with the Indians. You cannot work with animistic people and not believe there is a real battle going on.

The next day Joseph's dad (who was president of his mission agency) told me what was going on and said, "Will you just talk to Joseph about this thing? He heard this spirit saying, 'Just open yourself up, Joseph, I'll come in.' Of course, he didn't want to do that."

I was thinking, *What will I say to this little guy?* I didn't know what to say, but I agreed to talk to Joseph.

So after I spoke the next morning, Joseph and I walked over to the motor home their family was staying in for the meetings. As we were going up the steps, he turned to me and said, "You know, Mr. Logan, I have big problems. Are you good at this?" I almost had to smile.

"I'm learning," I said. So we went in and sat down. I was still praying inwardly, "Lord, I don't know what to say. I don't know how to approach this." Joseph was serious about it. He had a Bible, a notebook, and a pencil, ready to take notes. At age seven-and-a-half, he wanted answers.

As we sat there, a verse of Scripture came to me. I said, "You know, Joseph, 1 John 5:18b says when we're in Christ, the wicked one cannot touch us."

"You know, that's a good one," Joseph said.

"Yes, it really is, you ought to write it down." So he wrote the verse down. That broke it open for me, and from there the Lord gave me something that might help you if you ever have to deal with children in the area of spiritual warfare.

The one thing you don't want is for children to fear the enemy. They don't need to fear Satan for the same reason you and I don't have to fear him. He is defeated.

So I said, "Joseph, have you ever been to the snake house at the zoo?"

"Yes."

I acted shocked. "You mean you went into a snake house?"

"Sure."

"Really?" I wanted Joseph to think about it.

"Yes. Why?"

"But Joseph, there are poisonous snakes in there!"

"Yeah, Mr. Logan, but there's glass." And then he said, "Jesus is the glass, isn't He?"

"Yes, Joseph, Jesus is the glass. He's between you and the snake. Let's say we stayed in that zoo until it was dark. As we were walking out, we hear the lion roar. Would you be afraid?"

"Yeah, I think I would," he answered.

"What if I reminded you that the lion was behind bars?"

"Then I wouldn't be afraid."

This remarkable child then told me how the enemy had been harassing him. "What did you do when these temptations and thoughts came?" I asked.

"I did what my dad said. I said, 'In the name and authority of the Lord Jesus Christ, get out of here.'"

"What happened then?"

"The spirit left."

I know about a thousand adult Christians I wish understood spiritual warfare as clearly as Joseph does. He wasn't afraid even when the enemy tried to scare and intimidate him. I told him, "Joseph, God must have something wonderful for you to do."

He asked, "Why?"

"Because Satan is attacking you."

"What do you suppose God has for me, Mr. Logan?"

"Well, I'm not sure, but He'll show you. Why don't you dedicate your life to the Lord and His will for you right now?"

In a simple prayer, Joseph did just that, dedicating himself to God's will for his life. Later, this little guy ran up to his father with all these missionaries around and said, "Dad, guess what? God has something wonderful for me to do."

About three years later Joseph told me, "Mr. Logan, I think I know what God wants me to do. I have a pretty good voice. I think He wants me to be a singer."

Today, Joseph is one of my best prayer partners. He has been praying for me for more than nine years. I hear from his father every now and then. Joseph is doing great, and there's no doubt that God does indeed have something special for His very special child.

Spiritual attacks on children are an issue for children of those in full-time Christian service as much as children of dedicated Christian parents in other vocational callings. We should always treat with respect the questions our little ones have and the fears they raise, but never more than when those questions have to do with God's power and Satan's power.

Joshua

Joshua is another young man who can teach us a lot about confronting satanic influence. Joshua is autistic, totally unable to communicate verbally. All he can do is make noises, and he has little control over his body. He was born into the home of a godly pastor and his wife, whom we'll call the Smiths. The Smiths have six other children, all of whom are healthy. Joshua, however, began causing severe problems while he was still a young boy.

He would fly into violent fits of rage, during which he destroyed things and tried to hurt his little sisters. The family's life became so intolerable, and Joshua became so dangerous, that when he was about ten years old, his parents reluctantly committed him to a residential center.

Only a family that has experienced what Joshua's family went through can appreciate the agony involved in their decision. Joshua's parents loved him. He was a gift from God. But it seemed as if they had no other choice, because they had no reason to believe Joshua's behavior would ever improve.

Joshua stayed at the residential center for the next five years. His parents visited him frequently, but it wasn't enough to put their hearts at ease. Pastor Smith had a growing conviction, shared by his wife, that they needed to bring him back home and trust God for the daily grace it would take to cope with Joshua's rages.

When Joshua first came back home, the violent rages resumed. His siblings had to be aware of him constantly and try to stay out of his way. Joshua's parents prayed over him, read the Scriptures to him, and tried to discipline him. In time Joshua's behavior became manageable. But IQ tests showed that he was profoundly retarded, with an IQ of about 36.

When the Smiths told friends of their decision to bring Joshua home, some were bold enough to tell them they were crazy. Pastor Smith says the only reason he could come up with for taking this step was obedience to God. In January 1992, the family began to see the wisdom of God's leading.

At that time, Joshua's parents learned a technique called "facilitated communication." It involved holding Joshua's hand steady so he could push letters on a computer keyboard. Joshua's dad confesses he was skeptical. They had tried so many things to get through to Joshua. Besides, he had been told his son was "profoundly retarded."

But this time it was different. One day, Joshua stunned his mother by typing out this message: "I found God. Jesus died on the cross for me. I accepted Christ as my Savior six years ago." Mrs. Smith called her husband, who came racing home from his office at the church.

Hardly daring to believe what he heard, Pastor Smith took Joshua's hand and asked him what they had had for dinner the night before. To his amazement, Joshua typed "pizza."

This incident opened a floodgate of information from Joshua. He told his parents how lonely it was not to be able to communicate. He shared large passages of Scripture he had memorized and told of the books he had read. He told how he had learned to read by listening to his mother teach the younger children phonetics during home school sessions. Joshua also affirmed that he was not bitter about his condition, and affirmed his love for God and people.

This amazing discovery seemed to be the end of the Smiths' story. Joshua, who was seventeen by now, refused to take any more intelligence tests because he said they didn't accurately measure autistic people! Despite this, doctors and educators Joshua has worked with now believe he is a genius.

But Joshua's parents didn't know about Luke, a "friend" of Joshua's—and that's the rest of the story.

Just after the family made the discovery that Joshua could communicate, Pastor Smith received a recording of one of my messages on the subject of demon activity in believers. He played it at a family devotional time, but after about fifteen minutes he turned it off and asked his wife to throw it in the trash.

After all, I have two advanced degrees in theology, Pastor Smith told himself. *I'm a certified counselor. My theology doesn't allow for the possibility of significant enemy activity in the lives of God's people. Besides, only religious "kooks" dabble in the demonic.*

So the tape was thrown away, and Pastor Smith considered the case closed. But one day, Joshua typed out this message: "I can't find Luke. He is my special friend. I met him when we lived in [a city where his father once was a pastor]. He told me to hit the girls. He told me to break things."

Joshua went on to explain that Luke followed him to the residential center and then back home. "But after I received Christ, I felt Luke was not good for me," he wrote. Joshua would tell Luke to leave and he would—for a time. But he always returned.

Luke would tell Joshua that no one else loved him, that he needed to scare and hurt his sisters and tear up the house, and that he (Luke) would always be his friend. Joshua didn't really want Luke around, but he would get so lonely he would break down and ask Luke to return.

Needless to say, Pastor Smith was stunned. He finally came to believe what later proved to be true. "Luke" was an evil spirit, sent to be Joshua's "spirit guide" to influence him toward evil and destroy him and his family. All these years, this incredible spiritual battle had been raging in Joshua's life, and no one else knew. One day I got a call from Pastor Smith, and before long I visited this remarkable family.

Joshua and I talked a lot, and became good friends. He told me Luke first came to him when he was four. Luke could understand what Joshua was saying in his mind. They talked all the time. At first, Joshua liked Luke because Luke said he liked Joshua and wanted to be his friend.

HIGHER GROUND:
Helping Our Children

1. Ask your children if they see things no one else sees or hears things no one else hears. If so, have them explain what they see or hear. If they see anything coming out of a closet or a certain corner of a room, take the steps outlined in number 4 below.

2. If you suspect any enemy involvement in your children's lives, take your authority as a parent and command the enemy to leave your child alone and go where Jesus sends him. If your children are very young, you can pray over them as they sleep. That way, it isn't traumatic for them, and they don't know what's happening.

3. Pray God's hedge of protection around your children. The following outline is adapted from the Institute in Basic Life Principles. You may find it helpful. First, ask God to bind and rebuke the power of the enemy in the life of each family member. As we learned in Mark 3:27, Satan cannot spoil our houses unless he binds the "strong man." Second, pray in the name of and through the blood of the Lord Jesus Christ (note John 14:13).[1] Third, claim the Scripture that relates to the kind of protection needed. For example, for protection from sin claim Romans 6:14; for protection from discouragement claim Hebrews 13:5.

4. For children who are having night terrors, take two important steps. First, cleanse your home in prayer. Prayerfully walk through your home, asking God to reveal anything that can be used by the enemy to attack your family. Destroy suspicious items.[2]

   Second, explain to your children that God sees them and that they are never out of His sight or care (Genesis 16:13). Read Psalm 3:5 and 4:8 together (older children will also appreciate Psalm 127:2 and Proverbs 3:24, 26). Pray with your children that God will send His angels to guard them while they are sleeping and not allow the enemy to give them bad dreams.

5. Dedicate your home and the ground it stands on to the Lord, that it might be a lighthouse in your community. Ask God to help you create a godly atmosphere in your home.

But after Joshua became a Christian, he says he found out that Luke was lying to him when he said that neither God nor his parents loved him. I shared with Joshua's father some of the principles of spiritual warfare I've shared with you, and as the spiritual authority in his home, Pastor Smith commanded Luke in the name and authority of Christ to leave Joshua.

Joshua himself writes, "The moment I lost Luke is when Dad told him to leave. Dad is my authority. He had to obey Dad. I am glad. I feel clean. I feel good. I feel like God is all that I need. I am clean forever."

I don't have the space to tell you all the details of this incredible story. So many exciting things have happened. Joshua's story made the newspaper in a major city near where he lives.

Today, Joshua has had the opportunity to speak to groups of educators and graduate students. Because of his severe physical limitations Joshua could not attend public school, yet he proved to be a very able student as his mother taught him at home. Recently, the local school board has discussed the possibility of hiring him as a consultant on special education.

Joshua is also growing in his spiritual life, and he is one of my most faithful prayer partners. But I don't want you to think that Joshua has some sort of special exemption from God when it comes to spiritual warfare. He has to do the same things you and I do to walk in victory.

One example of this is the struggles Joshua had after his father dealt with Luke. Joshua discovered that he had the power to read other people's minds—a power he received from Luke. Joshua enjoyed telling visitors to his home things like the names of family members and other details he had no way of knowing. Needless to say, this power was very disconcerting to others and worrisome to Joshua's parents.

But Joshua says he enjoyed this power and didn't want to give it up. This should sound familiar. Remember Scott, the young man we met in chapter 3? He realized that if he renounced his occult involvement, he would lose his powers and be ordinary like everyone else.

Joshua had that same struggle, complicated by his feeling of living in his lonely "prison," his body. Here is part of an amazing letter Joshua wrote me about his struggle:

> It is wonderful to be free. I believe that I AM FREE. It is like a new life. I find that I STILL struggle. There are still attacks. I am disappointed when I sin. I know that I am forgiven. I know that I still struggle without sin overcoming me. It is hard sometimes. I love God.
>
> I find that I like power. It is hard to give up that power [to read minds]. I will do it because it is the right thing to do. It is hard. I find that . . . power is addictive. It takes the power of God to overcome the power addiction.

Isn't that profound? My point is that even though in many ways Joshua is an exceptional person, he came to freedom—and is living in freedom today—through the overcoming power of Christ. In this, he's no different than your children and mine.

By the way, as an autistic person who cannot speak and has other serious limitations, Joshua likens his "prison" to the apostle Paul's prison. Joshua says that like Paul, he can write to other people from prison and help them live the way God wants them to live. Praise God for His overcoming power!

Helping Your Children in Warfare

As a parent, there are several important things you can do to determine where your children are right now and what kind of help they may need in dealing with the enemy. I have summarized some action steps in "Helping Our Children" on page 150. Here are more specifics on how to help your children resist potential satanic attacks.

Observing and Asking

Any counselor will tell you that if you observe a sudden or drastic change in your child's attitudes or actions, something is amiss. This is true in the spiritual realm too. Children who are practicing any form of occult activity, for instance, will often exhibit strange or violent behavior. A young person who is under attack from the enemy may show a change in behavior or attitude. Joshua is a good example of this. Even though he couldn't tell anyone what was troubling him, his violent outbursts were a direct result of demonic activity.

With younger children, if you suspect any enemy involvement you can ask the child if he or she ever sees things no one else sees or hears things no one else hears. If the answer is yes, there are things you can do to deal with the problem. (See "Helping Our Children" for specifics.)

Before we go any further, I have to tell you about what happened to one family when the parents asked their children that question. Dad sat the boys down and asked them if they ever saw things no one else saw. They said no.

But when he asked them if they ever heard things no one else hears, they said yes, they heard voices all the time. Afraid of what he was going to find out, the father asked the boys where the voices were coming from. "We hear them out in the backyard" was the answer.

"Show me," dad said, so the boys took him out in the backyard.

As they stood there the boys said, "Listen, dad, there's the voice now."

The father strained to listen—and sure enough, there was this strange voice wafting through the air. It was coming from the loudspeaker at a new car dealership several blocks away!

Wielding the Weapon of Prayer

Not all cases of suspected enemy activity are solved so easily. That's why I'm grateful for the spiritual authority God gives us as parents in our children's lives. Probably the greatest weapon we have against Satan is one that is available to every Christian parent—the weapon of prayer. Specifically, we can pray God's hedge of protection around our children.

We talked about this concept in an earlier chapter, where we saw that Job interceded with God on behalf of his children and God placed a hedge around Job's family. This hedge was so effective against Satan that Satan himself complained to God, "Hast not thou made an hedge about him, and about his house, and about all that he hath on every side?" (Job 1:10). Praying God's hedge of protection around your children and/or grandchildren is a vital part of your spiritual warfare on their behalf. (Again, see "Helping Our Children" for specific ideas about such a prayer.)

As you consider such a prayer, however, please note that there is no specific formula or wording to follow in order to resist the devil. Prayer is not a magic wand we wave over the enemy. The important thing is the attitude of our hearts when we pray, not just the words we say. God wants us to come to Him in faith, believing that He is able to do far beyond what we could ask or even think (Ephesians 3:20).

— Part 3 —
Staying Free

— 12 —

WHO'S THE WINNER, WHO'S THE LOSER HERE?

I grew up in Los Angeles, so the annual New Year's Day Tournament of Roses parade in nearby Pasadena was a big event for us. One year I went to the parade with a friend. We stood on the street with thousands of other spectators straining to get a good look at the floats.

After one particularly beautiful float went by, receiving lots of oohs and ahs, we turned our heads to look at the next one. We waited, but nothing came. Thousands of people craned their necks looking up that road, but they saw nothing. We knew it was too early for the parade to be over, but from our vantage point it certainly looked like it was finished.

What we didn't know was that three blocks from where we were standing, a float had broken down. The people watching on television knew what was happening, of course, because there was a man with a television camera flying high above the parade in a helicopter.

That camera had a much better perspective of the parade than we had standing on the street. It allowed the audience to view the larger scene, so they knew exactly what was going on. If my friend and I and the people around us had acted from our perspective alone, we would have assumed the parade was over and gone home. The lesson is pretty obvious when it comes to my perspective versus God's. He sees the whole parade, so He knows what's happening at every point along the way. That's why I need His wisdom. I can't act on my perspective alone.

Wisdom is the ability to see life as God sees it. Aren't you glad He gives us wisdom as His children so we don't have to try and figure things out based on our limited perspective?

We know God wants us to operate in His wisdom because Paul prays that God will give Christians a "spirit of wisdom" (Ephesians 1:17). Why do we need God's wisdom? There are a lot of reasons, but let me suggest two in particular.

First, we need God's wisdom to understand who we are in Christ—what it means to be an heir with Him, to reign with Him, to experience His limitless power, and to be seated with Him "in the heavenly places." Until you grasp the position, privileges, and power that are yours in Christ, you will be a candidate for defeat in spiritual warfare.

Second, we need God's wisdom to see our enemy as he really is. I hope the message has come through already that when it comes to God's people, Satan is a defeated foe. He's a roaring lion, but all he has is his roar; he has no lasting bite. He has access to our lives, but he is a spirit of influence only. As we will see, Christ thoroughly defeated and disarmed Satan at the cross. That's why it's so tragic whenever the enemy convinces a believer that in his or her case, defeat and bondage are inevitable and irreversible. At those times, Satan's roar seems to be joined by a big bite, as a believer capitulates to his influence on earth.

Who You Are in Christ

In this chapter, which opens the final section of the book, I want to help you understand these two very important truths: who you are in Christ, and why the enemy is a defeated foe. Since we must have God's wisdom to see this, and since Paul prays for wisdom on our behalf, let's begin with the apostle's prayer in Ephesians 1:15–23.

You are God's Child

There is much more in these wonderful verses than we can cover in this limited space. But several verses deserve highlighting, as they are especially helpful and relevant to the issue of spiritual warfare. In this passage we learn we have the privileges of being God's children, having God's power in our lives, being on the winning side, and being able to walk in victory.

Notice first that the wisdom Paul prays for in verse 17 is the kind of wisdom that yields a knowledge of God. As a child of God, your primary calling is to get to know your Father, not the enemy. We are never told to know Satan in the way we are told to know God.

As I said before, I'm not overly curious about the things of evil. Satan is not the focus of my time and attention. I want to be aware of my enemy and understand his attacks so I can stand against him, but I don't want to know any more about Satan's works and ways than I need to know to defeat him and help other believers do the same. We are to keep our eyes on Jesus (Hebrews 12:1–2).

You Have God's Power

The greatest verse on God's power in the entire New Testament may be Ephesians 1:19. Paul prays that we will understand "what is the exceeding greatness of [God's] power to us-ward who believe, according to the working of his mighty power." Why does Paul use all of these superlatives to describe God's power? I think God is saying to us through the apostle, "Don't put a limit on My power. Don't box Me in. Watch what I can do."

How great is this power we have available to us, then? It's great enough to bring a dead man back to life! That's what verse 20 says. God's power was supremely on display when He raised Christ from the dead.

Don't miss the point. The same power God used to raise His Son is the power He gives you and me to live a victorious Christian life. I can't even imagine how much power it took to raise Jesus from the dead, can you? That's the power we are to stand in day by day.

What a far cry this is from the impression we often get that spiritual warfare and resisting the enemy is a matter of gritting my teeth and hanging on for dear life. That's trying to stand against Satan and live the Christian life in the flesh. It never has worked, and it never will work.

You're on the Winning Side

It gets even better. Paul reminds us that after God raised Jesus from the dead, He set His Son "at his own right hand in the heavenly places" (Ephesians 1:20b). A person can't sit down until the work is finished. Jesus has sat down, so this is a picture of completed work.

Jesus is not battling the spirit world on our behalf today in the sense that there's any doubt about the outcome. The conquest has already been made. He is presently enthroned "far above" any other power (v. 21). We'll see in Ephesians 6 (which I deal with in chapter 14) that these authorities Paul names include demonic entities who work in assigned realms.

So what we have here is not only a vivid picture of Christ's finished work, but a picture of total defeat for the kingdom of darkness. In the ancient world, the victor in battle would take the highest ranking officer of the defeated forces, lay him down, and put his foot on his throat, the most vulnerable part of the body. It was a gesture of abject defeat for the loser. The victor would also strip the enemy army of its weapons and parade the defeated soldiers through the streets, saying in effect, "Look, the enemy you feared has been defeated. He has no weapons. You don't have to be afraid of him anymore."

That's what Christ has done with our enemy! Satan and all of his forces are under the feet of Christ (v. 22). If you are seated with Christ, that means the enemy is under your feet too. Freedom is our birthright in Christ. It grieves Him when we don't claim and walk in our birthright.

You Can Walk in Victory

I'm not saying that because we're on the winning side, the battle is easy. This book makes it clear that we are in a serious spiritual battle. Even though freedom and victory are our birthright, we must stay on the alert. Getting free is easy, staying free is hard.

Walking in victory is the hard part. But it can be done, and I don't know any better illustration of this truth than the lives of great Christians. Our family has read hundreds of missionary biographies, and we've seen this over and over. An outstanding example of someone who really understood his position in Christ and acted on it is the great missionary John Paton. His autobiography tells of his thirty years among cannibals in the New Hebrides Islands in a pioneering ministry.

Paton and his wife arrived at one of the islands in 1858, but she died in childbirth the next year. For his remaining years, Paton was in constant danger from these cannibals. In *Thirty Years with South Sea Cannibals*, Paton describes one day when the cannibals tried to attack him. He began to flee as the natives charged him, screaming and hollering. One tribesman hurled his tomahawk at Paton, but just as he released the weapon, Paton's foot caught in a log, he fell flat, and the tomahawk thudded into the tree over his head. Paton then ran to safety.

Another time, Paton was weeding his garden when a cannibal aimed a musket on him. Paton knew the cannibal had trained the weapon on him but kept going down the row weeding. The cannibal kept following him. For some reason, the cannibal chose not to fire. Later someone asked, "How could you do that?"

Paton replied, "You know, if my life is over, it's over. And if it's not, I better weed the garden." God would not allow that cannibal to shoot Paton unless it was His time, and if it wasn't God's time, Paton had things to do.

I remember how I would read a chapter of Paton's book each night to my son, Richard, when he was almost four years old. Richard would then go to bed, and he'd look up and say, "Oh Dad, isn't God wonderful?"

That truth is exactly what I wanted to instill in all my children, the truth that God is wonderful and that if we are in Christ, we have no need to fear the enemy. It's a truth you can claim too. Satan cannot touch us unless the Father permits it, because we are in Christ.

Ruth Paxson makes an important distinction in her classic book on Ephesians, *The Wealth, Walk and Warfare of the Christian.* I love how she puts it:

> To who did Paul write this epistle and to who is it addressed? He wrote it to saints at Ephesus but addressed it to the faithful in Christ. Their temporary residence was *at Ephesus,* which was the center of idolatry, superstition, luxury and vice. . . . Yet their real abode was *in Christ,* which was to them the center of worship, light, life, and holiness. . . . Oh, my friend, where do you live—at or in?

She's right: The issue is not where you're at, but who you are in. What a privilege is ours to be seated in Christ at God's right hand "far above" everything, sharing His victory and power over the forces of darkness.

God Shall Deliver You

Let me leave you with another positive truth before we turn to the subject of Satan's defeat at Calvary. In 2 Timothy 4:18 Paul writes, "The Lord shall deliver me from every evil work, and will preserve me unto His heavenly kingdom: to whom be glory for ever and ever."

That's a wonderful promise, that God will deliver us from Satan's evil work. But actually, this promise is even more thrilling than that. The King James Version doesn't really capture the idea here. The New International Version better reflects the Greek by translating "work" as "attack." It reads, "The Lord will rescue me from every evil attack."

Isn't that tremendous? What a promise. The Lord will deliver or rescue me from every attack of the enemy and bring me into His heavenly kingdom. This is a promise of victory in spiritual warfare for every man and woman who is in Christ.

Your Defeated Foe

A pastor from the Midwest wrote me recently of the newfound freedom and spiritual victory in his ministry. He is now full of joy, and it has affected much of his ministry. He explained how his freedom has revitalized one particular ministry, his counseling:

> After years of personal bondage and defeat, my theology began to reflect my own experience that lasting victory was not possible on this side of glory.
>
> My counseling ministry resembled a boxing coach in the corner of the ring watching my guys get beat up. Between rounds the people would come into my office for counsel. My goal was to stop the bleeding, pat them on the back to cheer them up, give them a few verses of encouragement, and then send them back out to get beat up

HIGHER GROUND:
Resting in Christ

Christ has achieved the victory over Satan at the cross, and as His followers we can have victory over Satan's influence. Here are four steps to finding rest through Christ by letting Him lead us.

1. Ask yourself how you perceive God dealing with you as His child. Do you see your relationship with God in terms of your performance? If so, you are probably a performance-oriented person, one who is at times driven to do "religious" things, believing that if you do all of these things (usually to perfection), you will feel loved and accepted by God. If this describes you, turn to Romans 5:8 and Ephesians 1:6 and read the truth again—the truth that while you were still a sinner Christ died for you, and that you are already accepted in Him.

2. Read Psalm 23:1–2 and John 10:3–4, which remind us that Jesus as the Good Shepherd leads His sheep, not drives them. Recognize that the feeling of "I just have to do more" is not of God, and ask His forgiveness for not resting in the finished work of Christ. Also, ask God to free you from trying to achieve by the works of the flesh what has already been provided by Christ on the cross.

3. Tell God you will no longer try to earn His love and acceptance. Instead, because He loves and accepts you, tell Him you will serve Him.

4. Enter into the rest Christ has for you and, from that place of rest, serve Him.

again. My punch line was, "If you must fall, do so victoriously." How deceived I was! What a joy [now] to lead others to lasting freedom. I recognize that they are still in a boxing match, but they are fighting a defeated foe. Jesus dealt the knockout blow at Calvary, and by faith I enter into His victory.

Once this pastor realized that Satan is already a defeated foe, he realized that he was not fighting to gain the victory, but was fighting from a position of victory. There is all the difference in the world between those two approaches to the Christian life.

Defeated at the Cross

That is a crucial aspect of spiritual warfare I teach my clients under satanic attack, and one we all need to remember: Satan has already been defeated at the cross. Several passages of Scripture discuss this defeat. The first I want to look at is Colossians 2:13–15. This passage is probably the most important on the subject, especially verse 15. In fact I think these three verses should be printed in your Bible in gold.

Paul tells us that Jesus dealt with three important things in His death on the cross. The first two were our sins (v. 13) and the requirements of the law (v. 14). We were "dead" in our sins, which means we couldn't do anything about them. But Jesus "quickened" us—made us alive in Him—by forgiving us "all trespasses." The sentence of death for our sins was removed from us and placed on Jesus. Through the cross, the Savior also fulfilled the requirements of the Law, which released us from its bondage (v. 14). This "handwriting of ordinances" was a written acknowledgment of debt made in the handwriting of the debtor. The Mosaic law put us in debt to God. But He canceled that debt, nailing it to the cross. Jesus paid it all.

The third victory Jesus accomplished on the cross is in verse 15, and it's the one we need to focus on. Here Paul outlines the fatal blow that Christ's death dealt to the demonic world: "And having spoiled principalities and powers, he made a shew of them openly, triumphing over them in it." The "it," of course, is Christ's death, which to all outward appearances was a defeat not for Satan, but for Jesus Himself.

But thankfully, appearances don't count in the spiritual world. Jesus "spoiled" demonic principalities in His death; that is, He disarmed the demonic world. He took away their weapons.

Then, Jesus put these defeated powers on open display. Just as a conquering general paraded his defeated enemies through the streets, Jesus put the vanquished forces of hell on parade. We no longer need to fear these defeated foes. Another reason to put a conquered enemy on public display was to remind people that their allegiance was not to the losing army, but to the one on the horse, the conqueror.

The lesson for us is obvious. Our allegiance is to our conqueror on the white horse, the Lord Jesus Christ. This truth has tremendous implications for the final days too, because we know that He will ride forth someday to conquer (Revelation 19:11–16).

Colossians 2:15 also tells us that Jesus marched in triumph over Satan and his forces. This completes the picture of utter defeat for the demonic world. Jesus accomplished all of this while hanging in weakness and shame on a Roman cross—hardly the epitome of the conquering hero. But His power was not dependent on what was seen. We can praise God for that.

Three Questions

The truth of Jesus Christ's triumph over Satan raises at least three questions in my mind. The first is, Why did the demonic world push so hard to have Jesus crucified if the cross was the instrument of their defeat?

I believe this is answered best in 1 Corinthians 2:6–8, a passage I didn't understand for years because I didn't believe in the reality of the spirit world. Paul says the "princes of this world" (vv. 6, 8) did not understand what the outcome of Christ's death would be, or they never would have moved people to crucify Him.

There may be some debate as to whether Paul has earthly or spiritual authorities in mind here. I'm convinced he's referring to demonic rulers. The fact is that even though Jesus was crucified at the hands of Jewish and Gentile authorities, they were demonically inspired. The plot against Him was hatched in the pit of hell. There's no doubt about this.

Paul's explanation proves that Satan is not all-knowing and all-powerful. He did not know that the cross meant his defeat. God displayed His wisdom "in a mystery" (v. 7, see also Ephesians 3:9), the mystery of the cross.

In light of Colossians 2 and 1 Corinthians 2, it's interesting to turn to Luke 22, a chapter that we looked at earlier in another setting. Verses 52–53 make it clear that the demonic world wanted Jesus dead. He said Himself in the Garden of Gethsemane that this was the hour for "the power of darkness" to reign.

Look back at Luke 22:3. Satan himself entered Judas. The betrayal of Christ was too big a job to trust to an underling. Satan covered all of his bases . . . except one. He had no control over the power of God—and God confounded the powers of hell by turning the cross into a triumph.

Here's a second question that occurs to me, and maybe to you too. If Satan is a defeated enemy, stripped of his weapons and put on public display, why is everything such a mess? Paul provides the answer in Colossians 1:13: We have been delivered from the power of darkness—not the presence of darkness. Satan is still able to influence men and women toward evil, for a season, at least. "The whole world lieth in wickedness [or, "the wicked one]," John says (1 John 5:19).

So as long as we live every day in a wicked world, we will see and feel its ugly results. Satan is defeated in the lives of believers only. He's got the unsaved world in his grip. But we need to keep reminding ourselves that Satan's only power in our lives is in the lie. That's all he's got to work with.

Let me ask a third question, one that's harder to answer. Why are there so many losers on the winning team? Why are so many Christians living defeated lives? I don't have a problem understanding why my unsaved neighbor lives in defeat and spiritual bondage. He doesn't know any better. But what bothers me is why so many Christians are struggling to have spiritual victory.

My desire in this book is twofold: (1) to show that moral and spiritual defeat is not inevitable for the believer, and (2) to help God's people come to complete freedom in Christ and walk in daily victory. As someone has said, if we turn to the last chapter of Revelation we find out how it all ends: in victory for Christ and His followers. If we're the winners in the end because we belong to Christ, why can't we live as winners today? The power is there, all the power we could ever need to make right choices.

I'm not talking about the kind of "victory" some people advocate, where you ride the clouds all the time and never acknowledge any pain or problem. You can't get past the book of Job with that theology. Job was morally pure, honest, concerned about God's reputation, and he hated evil.

Some Christians think a godly man like that isn't going to get any flak from the enemy. But that's wrong. Who brought up Job to Satan? God did! Being on the winning team doesn't mean you are excused from the battle.

Strategies of the Deceiver

Remembering two important truths from the Scriptures can help us in overcoming Satan's influence in our lives. First, Satan's methods often use bondage to trip us up in our devotion to Christ. Second, Satan's methods feature deceit and lies.

Religious Bondage

The final verses of Colossians 2 reveal something interesting about Satan's strategies in spiritual warfare. After recounting Christ's total victory over the forces of darkness in verses 13–15, Paul says "therefore" (v. 16, NIV), and he describes some of the implications of what he has just said. In verses 16–23, the apostle discusses various forms of religious bondage. In other words, since we've been forgiven and made alive with Christ, and our eternal destiny is secure, and since Satan was soundly defeated at the cross, he only has one tactic left to trip us up. He wants to lead us into bondage to someone or something other than Christ.

These verses remind us that Satan isn't too particular about what form that bondage takes. If he can't ensnare you sexually, emotionally, or financially or by some form of perversion, he'll ensnare you in religious bondage. The results are the same: you're rendered powerless and useless to the Lord. And results are all that the enemy cares about.

That's the danger the Colossian believers faced, and it's still a danger for us today. Isn't it typical of Paul to go straight from the heights of glorious eternal or positional truth right down to the nitty-gritty of daily life? He does that for a very good reason. Truth should impact and shape our lives now.

The Deceiver and Liar

Second, the Scriptures show us again and again a truth mentioned earlier: Because Satan is defeated, his only real power is in the lie.

He's a deceiver who wants to trap you and me in self-deception (Galatians 6:3; James 1:22; 1 John 1:8), deception by others (Ephesians 5:6; 2 Timothy 3:13; 2 John 7), and in his own work of deception (1 Timothy 1:4; Revelation 12:9).

But the operative word when it comes to Satan is *defeated.* He's the loser, which makes you the winner in Christ. Let's live according to that victory, in the power of our great victor, Jesus Christ.

— 13 —
LEARNING TO LIVE LIKE A WINNER

Now that we know we're on the winning team in Christ, we need to understand how to live like a winner. As I suggested in the last chapter, it's not always easy to tell the winners from the losers when you look around. That's because even though Satan is a defeated enemy, he's still in there fighting. And even though he knows the war is lost, he still wins a lot of battles against God's people. Why is this, given the power Christ has and given that we are seated with Him?

I believe it goes back to something I mentioned earlier: the fact that many Christians have never once resisted the devil in spiritual warfare. Yet as we have seen in James 4:7, we are told to "resist the devil."

Recognizing the Tempter

This chapter will deal in-depth with what it means to "resist the devil." I've shared this material with thousands of missionaries, pastors, other Christian workers, and laypeople around the world, and many have told me how much it helped them to see how the enemy works and how we can stand against him. I hope you'll find practical help here for your daily Christian life, because spiritual warfare is not the exception, but the rule for the child of God. The apostle Paul said that all of us wrestle against demonic spirits (see Ephesians 6:12).

In chapter 12 we asked some tough questions; let me begin this chapter with several more. How can we resist an enemy we can't see if we don't know he's there? Why is it we don't recognize his temptations until after we fail? That seems a little bit late. Do we have to be lying in the ditch before we realize, "I think I've just come to grips with the enemy"?

We want to deal with these issues so we can get on the front side of temptation, before we get run off the road and wind up in the ditch. But to do this we've got to know how Satan operates, because he usually doesn't knock and say, "Logan, this is the devil. I'm here to wipe you out today."

We'll find some answers to our questions in the book of James, a portion of Scripture I thank God for day after day. The reason we don't recognize the enemy's involvement in temptation is found in James 1:12–14:

> Blessed is the man that endureth temptation: for when he is tried, he shall receive the crown of life, which the Lord hath promised to them that love him. Let no man say when he is tempted, I am tempted of God: for God cannot be tempted with evil, neither tempteth he any man: but every man is tempted, when he is drawn away of his own lust, and enticed.

The first thing James tells us is that if we endure temptation, it's a sign that we love the Lord Jesus (v. 12). The second thing is that if we are tempted to do evil, we can know it's not from God, because He does not tempt us. God tries or tests us to draw us to Himself, while Satan tempts us to draw us away from God and to himself.

God's Tests

This is so important. How do you know if what you're facing is a temptation from the enemy or a test from God? A question to ask yourself is, *If I give in to these thoughts, if I go ahead and do them, will I find myself being drawn closer to the Lord, or being pulled away from Him?* If the situation is a test from God, you will be spiritually stronger if you follow the leading of your heart.

Now you and I can fail God's test, and the failure may draw us away from Him. But that's an entirely different matter than yielding to sin. The goal of God's testing is to draw us into a deeper, closer walk with Him.

God's Revelation

After God tests us, He often reveals aspects of His character we would have never known if we hadn't gone through the test. Just ask Abraham. If Abraham had failed the test in the offering of Isaac on Mount Moriah, he would never have known God as *Jehovah Jireh,* "the Lord will provide" (Genesis 22:14). But because Abraham endured the test, God revealed to him His character as the Provider for His people.

Haven't you had this happen to you? You go through some test, and you see God's sufficiency in a way you had never seen it before. Looking back over our family life, I'm thankful for the tests God has put the Logan family through. There are many of them I wouldn't ever want to repeat, but God was faithful and we learned something new and wonderful about Him each time.

One test I wouldn't want to repeat was the time we thought our second daughter, Terri, then just a baby, was dying. We didn't know what to do. The one thing we were afraid to do was give her to the Lord. We wrestled with this, but finally we got on our knees and said, "Lord, you can take our little girl if that's what You want to do." It was the hardest thing we ever did.

The most awful thoughts would come. *Here I am in Bible school, preparing to serve God. That's what happens, you know. You're going to serve God, and your little girl gets sick and is going to die.*

Yes, I was accusing God. Do you know where those thoughts came from? Can you smell the brimstone? I can now, but at that time I didn't recognize it. I didn't understand the enemy, didn't realize that he put those thoughts there. I was struggling with God. Here I was ready to be His servant, and He was going to take my daughter. I thought, *That's what you get. You might as well just go back.*

God saw fit not to take our daughter. Now I understand that the temptation to doubt God, to question His goodness and character, and to throw in the towel was not from Him—no temptation to doubt and discouragement ever is.

Understanding the Enemy's Temptations

On the contrary, James says in verse 14 that all of us are tempted when we are "drawn away of [our] own lust, and enticed."

No One Is Exempt

Notice first that "every" person is tempted. That underscores what Paul said about our wrestling with the forces of evil in spiritual warfare. No Christian is exempt from the battle.

Temptation Is Well-Aimed

Also, James says every one of us is tempted in exactly the same way. Not in exactly the same things, but in the same way—through our lusts.

Before we can hope to recognize and resist Satan's involvement in our temptations, we have to understand how he works. Satan only tempts us to do what we would secretly do anyway. Otherwise, it's no temptation. It doesn't have any appeal to us.

All of us are vulnerable to temptation. Satan knows your combination, and mine too. So when I'm tempted, it seems so normal that I don't recognize the one behind it. He's only asking me to do what I'm weak at anyway. I don't recognize the true source of the temptation because what I'm being tempted to do does not seem unusual, or "off the wall," for me.

Again, what may tempt others may not tempt you, but you can be sure Satan will tempt you in your vulnerable areas. When I'm counseling with or teaching men, I make this point by asking them a question: "If you were standing on a street corner in downtown Sioux City [or their hometown] and you suddenly got the thought to drop your pants, what would you do?"

Invariably, the men laugh and say, "Nothing." Why? Because for most of them, that's such an off the wall thing to do they wouldn't even consider it.

But do you know what? For some men I've dealt with, that temptation wouldn't be a cause for laughter. They would think about it. Their hands would sweat. They would have to fight hard not to do it. Why? Because they are battling a form of sexual bondage that makes actions like that seem appealing.

Or consider four men riding along in a car. All of a sudden they pass an adult bookstore. The two men in the front seat have been to stores like this one. Going there is a tremendous battle for them. The two guys in the back seat have never had a problem with pornography.

So guess what happens? While the two guys in the front seat are checking out the address, the guys in the back seat are saying, "Look at that place. Someone ought to burn it down." To these men, it's not a temptation; it's an eyesore and detestable.

Don't Judge Others

As you consider the nature of temptation, let me give one important caution. Consider again the four men who are driving by the adult bookstore. The two in the back seat abhor pornography and can't understand why anyone would mess with it. But let's suppose these same two men just happen to have tremendous problems with lust for material things. They'd do or sacrifice almost anything to get ahead, to be able to have a new car, better clothing, or a larger house.

Do you know what most of us have a tendency to do? If we're the kind of person who goes after money, we look down our noses at the people who use pornography. They're the bad guys. And the pornography users reason that at least they're not cheating or hurting someone else by looking at a few pictures. We all tend to justify our particular sin. Remember, we are neither to judge others nor think ourselves superior because of the areas in which we are immune to temptation. As Paul warns, we are to "take heed lest [we] fall" (1 Corinthians 10:12).

Knowing What to Resist

Interestingly, we are never told in the Bible to resist temptation. Do you know of a verse that says we should resist temptation? No, the Bible always tells us to resist the tempter.

The Wrong Focus

Why is this? Because if we try to resist the temptation, what are we looking at? The very thing that wipes us out.

One week I spoke on the principles of spiritual warfare with a particular mission group. Before arriving, I had decided I was going to lose weight during the conference, which I thought would be easy because everyone knows missionaries don't get paid much and the meals probably would be simple. Then one day at the conference I'm walking through the meal line and find my mouth start to water. *Satan must have cooked the desserts here last night,* I told myself. There before my eyes was this piece of strawberry pie with whipped cream on it. And it was free. What could I do?

I stood there for a minute looking at the pie, trying to resist it. But looking at it and saying "I won't, I won't," didn't work. That's like saying, "Let's go to Dairy Queen and resist sundaes." It cannot work. The focus is on the wrong thing, the very thing that trips me up. God doesn't want me to focus on that, because He knows if I keep looking long enough, I'm in trouble. That's why He says, "Resist the one behind the temptation. Resist the tempter, and he will flee."

The Right Focus

Let me give you an illustration of how we are to resist, using our great example, Jesus. He shows that we resist with God's truth, the Scripture. In Luke 4 we read that He was tempted even though he was filled with the Spirit: "And Jesus being full of the Holy Ghost returned from Jordan, and was led by the Spirit into the wilderness, being forty days tempted of the devil" (vv. 1–2a).

Notice that Jesus was led by the Spirit into the wilderness for one purpose: to be tempted. So we learn something very important and encouraging right off. It's no sin to be tempted. Jesus was tempted in "all points" like we're tempted (Hebrews 4:15), except that He did not sin.

What Satan does, though, is tell us, "You thought about it. You might as well do it." That's right out of the pit, because it may not have been my thought at all, but an intruding thought from him. That means I don't have to entertain it or act on it.

HIGHER GROUND:
Resisting Satan

When it comes to spiritual victory in our lives, we must remember that we are in a battle that is not against "flesh and blood" but spiritual evil forces (Ephesians 6:12). We must resist Satan. Here are ways to resist effectively.

1. Humble yourself before God (James 4:6). Acknowledge your need of grace (divine empowering) and guidance. Pray as David did in Psalm 23:3, "Father, lead me in the right paths, for Your reputation is at stake."

2. Submit yourself to God (James 4:7). Dedicate your body to glorifying God (1 Corinthians 6:19–20), your mind to thinking His thoughts (Philippians 4:8), your emotions to loving Him (Matthew 22:37), and your will to serving as unto God and not unto men (Ephesians 6:6–7).

3. Actively resist the devil (James 4:7). Come against Satan using the name of our Lord Jesus Christ (Philippians 2:9–11) and standing in His finished work on the cross. Read Revelation 12:11 and note the ways the saints overcame Satan. Identify the bait Satan is using to trap you (2 Timothy 2:26, see chapter 7). Use specific Scriptures against the temptation (Luke 4:4, 8, 12).

4. Counterattack (Ephesians 6:18–20). Select prayer targets for each area of attack, and pray that these people will do great harm to Satan and his kingdom.

5. Draw near to God (James 4:8). "Cleanse your hands," asking forgiveness for any violation of God's standards. "Purify your hearts," because the enemy uses our secret dreams and our double-mindedness against us. Use Psalm 139:23–24 as a guide for your prayers.

6. Get back in the race (Hebrews 12:1–2). Fix your gaze upon Christ and glance at the path for Satan's traps. To help you here, I highly recommend Joseph Carroll's book, *How to Worship Jesus Christ* (see the bibliography).

Peter (Matthew 16:23) and Ananias and Sapphira (Acts 5:3) had intruding thoughts from Satan. The problem was that they didn't resist those thoughts, and it cost the latter two their lives. Ananias and Sapphira were judged because they acted on Satan's thoughts, not because they had them.

In Luke 4:3 we read that Satan spoke to the Lord Jesus. Did Jesus hear what Satan said to Him? Yes, He did, and He heard Satan's wrong advice. We know that because He answered each temptation specifically. Thus Jesus received wrong thoughts.

But notice that *Jesus never acted on those wrong thoughts.* He thoroughly renounced them, as a matter of fact. My point is that receiving a wrong thought does not make me a sinner. It's what I do with it. In order for me to be tempted, the temptation has to register in my mind. There is a difference between an intruding thought and my thinking. Sin will be conceived only if I make the enemy's intruding thought part of my thinking.

Notice that when Jesus resisted the enemy the first time, Satan didn't flee, did he? He came at Jesus again, and Jesus resisted him a second time with Scripture, and then a third time. Wrestling the enemy is not just a little skirmish, a little side show. Satan often will persist; our job is to resist, in the power of God's Word and in the strength of the Spirit.

Look how skillfully Jesus used Scripture to defeat the devil. We know that all Scripture is inspired and profitable. So when Jesus was tempted by the enemy, why didn't He just say, "In the beginning God created the heavens and earth"? Isn't that Scripture? Isn't it profitable? Yes, but it didn't deal with the problem at hand. Jesus used specific Scriptures for specific temptation.

The second thing you need to know is that Jesus did not quote Scripture word for word. I believe this is an example of the use of the Greek word *rhema,* which like *logos* also means "word." We'll talk more about this when we discuss the Christian's armor in Chapter 14, because the "Word of God" in Ephesians 6:17 is *rhema.*

Basically this word means that we can use the truth of God's Word at the moment it's needed. Jesus and Satan were not having a Scripture-quoting contest. Jesus countered temptation with the truth of Scripture, and that's what mattered. If you can quote every verse word perfectly, that's great. But it's not necessary in the heat of spiritual battle.

Temptation: An Empowering Experience

When Jesus' temptation was finished, He "returned in the power of the Spirit into Galilee" (Luke 4:14). What a wonderful progression here. Jesus was filled with the Spirit, He underwent tremendous temptation and resisted successfully in the power of the Spirit, and he returned empowered by the very Spirit He was filled with.

Did you know that temptation can be one of the most empowering experiences of your life when you stand your ground and resist Satan in the power of the Spirit? You don't need to be afraid of an encounter with the enemy.

What we're talking about here is the opposite of a "grab the bed-post" battle where you hang on by grit and determination. Can you have a measure of victory over temptation in the power of the flesh? Yes, you can. I know alcoholics and former drug addicts who have gone through various programs and don't drink or use drugs anymore. But they are not Christians.

It is possible for us to have victory with grit and determination. But if the enemy tempts the flesh and you have victory over it in the flesh, guess who won? The flesh. And if you fail and fall back, guess who won? The flesh wins either way.

How to Resist the Devil

Thankfully, as Christians we don't have to resist Satan in the power of the flesh. God has provided a better way. Before we look at some biblical instructions for resisting Satan, it will help to note some general truths about resisting temptation.

First, we need to see that when we resist the enemy, we are standing against an outward attack. The enemy is on the outside. When someone in the New Testament was demonized, Jesus cast the spirit or spirits out of that person.

But if the evil spirits were attacking from the outside, Jesus didn't cast them out. He resisted them. So as we do battle with the enemy outside, if we resist him with truth, what will he do? He will go. Wouldn't it be neat if resisting only once would do it? But that wasn't the case even with Jesus. Satan is always looking for his opportune time.

Second, it's encouraging to know that sometimes, after we have gone through a real battle, God will put a special hedge of protection around us for a while. Then He lifts it so we can wrestle again and learn to stand. He protects us in that battle, and then He'll let us wrestle again.

Draw Near to God

We return to the book of James, this time to chapter 4, and look at the apostle's instructions for resisting. The first one I want to notice is in verse 8, which tells us what to do after we have gone through a time of temptation: "Draw nigh to God, and he will draw nigh to you."

That's exactly the opposite of what we are naturally inclined to do after battling temptation. We think, "Oh, that was so terrible. My thoughts were so bad. I'm so embarrassed. I just want to hide from God." But God wants us to draw close to Him. Isn't that beautiful?

So often we see in Scripture that the thing God tells us to do is the complete opposite of what we would normally do. For example, it is not normal for a man to love his wife the way he should. That's why God commanded him to do it. It's unnatural. It's not natural for a woman to submit to her husband. If it was, God wouldn't have mentioned it. But He commanded it.

So at the very time when you feel most inclined to pull away from God, He urges you to draw close. If you will do that, what will He do? He'll draw close to you. That's why I say that temptation can be a very empowering experience. Instead of separating you from the Lord, it can give you a very sweet time with Him.

Cleanse Your Heart

James continues in 4:8: "Cleanse your hands, ye sinners." Do you know what that speaks of to me? It means I got a little dirty in the battle and I need to ask God for cleansing. What cleanses the dirt of sin off my hands? The blood of Christ (1 John 1:9).

Next, at the end of verse 8, James tells us to deal with our secret desires. "Purify your hearts, ye double minded." A double-minded person is one who wants to walk with God and yet not deal with his secret desires—the very things the enemy uses to tempt him.

We have to deal very firmly with these desires. The process can be painful, as James acknowledges when he urges us, "Be afflicted, and mourn, and weep: let your laughter be turned to mourning, and your joy to heaviness" (v. 9).

Humble Yourself

When we have done that, we are ready to humble ourselves "in the sight of the Lord" (v. 10). What does He do in response? Push our faces in the dirt? No, He lifts us up!

"Submit yourselves therefore to God. Resist the devil," James tells us in 4:7. Then he tells us how to resist: by drawing near to God, purifying our hearts of sin and secret desires, and humbling ourselves before Him. It's a winning strategy every time, because it's God's strategy!

A Serious Wrestling Match

In the next chapter we will consider how to prepare for battle by wearing spiritual armor. For now, let's consider the imagery Paul had in mind when he said we wrestle against forces we cannot see: "We wrestle not against flesh and blood, but against principalities, against powers, against the rulers of the darkness of this world, against spiritual wickedness in high places. Wherefore take unto you the whole armour of God" (Ephesians 6:12–13).

Paul described a kind of wrestling far different than most televised wrestling today, which is really nothing more than entertainment, a sideshow. Hulk Hogan and some other hunk throw each other out of the ring while everybody is screaming. But in Paul's day, wrestling matches were serious, grim events. Usually, two slaves would wrestle in a final match until one of them could no longer get up. The winner would then climb to his feet and put his foot on the neck of the loser. He would call for a sword and flick out the eyes of the loser, who would walk in darkness the rest of his life as a reminder that he lost the wrestling match.

Why would a wrestler risk blindness like that? Because the slave who won was set free along with his family. Their names were inscribed on the wall of city, he never had to pay taxes again, and his children would have access to the finest education. It was worth the risk.

When you and I wrestle principalities and powers in the demonic realm, there's a lot at stake too. If we lose, if we fail to resist, we fall into sin that breaks our spiritual fellowship with the Father and can lead us into increasing spiritual attacks and bondage.

Have you been losing your battles with temptation? Let me encourage you to get alone with the Lord and pray, "Lord, show me where I'm vulnerable." It could be worry; it could be bitterness. I don't know what your temptation "hot buttons" are, but I know who does—the enemy of your soul. So does the Lord, and He can show you what they are so that you can be prepared to resist the tempter when he comes.

The best form of resistance is the one Jesus used, the Word. Find specific Scriptures that speak to your need and be ready to use them when Satan comes against you. You can resist the tempter and walk in the light.

There is a sin that easily besets us (Hebrews 12:1). We all have it. I wish I could get rid of mine, but God has not seen fit to remove it. But He says, "Jim, I'll give you something better. I'll give you more grace" (see James 4:6). Remember, "Resist the devil, and he will flee from you."

— 14 —
WHAT TO WEAR
TO THE BATTLE

I try not to read too much into the words of Scripture, but there are a few places where I can't help but wonder what was in the author's mind as he wrote.

One of those places is Ephesians 6:10, where Paul begins his teaching on spiritual warfare and the Christian's armor by saying, "Finally." I believe there's more behind that word than just a signal that Paul is coming to the final topic of the book. I think Paul is saying, "Finally, I can tell you what I wanted to tell you—which is how to fight spiritual warfare. But first, I had to get you spiritual, and it took five-and-one-half chapters to do that."

We're in much the same position in this book. There's so much I had to share with you before we could come to the point where we are ready to don our armor and fight a good fight for the mind. Now we are there. How do we apply the armor of God, by which we can "stand against the wiles of the devil"?

The Crux of the Battle

Ephesians 6 is the crux of the battle for spiritual warfare. Paul has prepared the Ephesians, and us, for this by saying don't grieve the Holy Spirit (Ephesians 4) and be filled with the Spirit (Ephesians 5). Now that our lives are under the control of the Holy Spirit, we are ready for warfare, ready to stand in victory. So let's look at the Christian's armor as we suit up for battle:

> Finally, my brethren, be strong in the Lord, and in the power of his might. Put on the whole armour of God, that ye may be able to stand against the wiles of the devil. For we wrestle not against flesh and blood, but against principalities, against powers, against the rulers of the darkness of this world, against spiritual wickedness in high places. Wherefore take unto you the whole armour of God, that ye

may be able to withstand in the evil day, and having done all, to stand. (vv. 10–13)

Our Demonic Enemies

In the previous chapter we discussed the concept of wrestling (v. 12a). Now let's consider the latter half of verse 12, where Paul mentions four groupings of demonic spirits we battle against. Before we can take up the armor, Paul wants us to know who we're fighting.

The first group is *principalities*. This is a very descriptive word. A prince is an appointed authority, and a *municipality* indicates a region of political governance. So these are demons appointed to govern over certain geographical areas in the kingdom of darkness.

We find support for this idea in the book of Daniel. The prophet was told by an angel that his prayer had been heard and answered, but that the angel was delayed in bringing the answer for twenty-one days by the "prince of the kingdom of Persia" (Daniel 10:12–13). That this was not a mere human is obvious from the fact that the archangel Michael had to be called upon for help. This "prince" was a demonic principality.

The second group Paul mentions is *powers*. These are demons who seek to have power over individual lives. They want to encroach on the lives of God's people. I once encountered a demon, which called himself "perversion," in a child just eight years old. The demon said he was just waiting for this boy to become sexual so he could destroy him.

When I was with my mission, another missionary took me with him one day to share the gospel with children who live in buildings owned by the New York City Port Authority. These were depressing places where the children lived in unbelievable degradation.

My fellow missionary worked often in these buildings. Before we went into the first one he said to me, "Jim, see if you can sense any dominant feeling as we go into these buildings." The first felt very bad; as we went through, there was just an overwhelming feeling of hopelessness. It was written on every face. In the next building, the overwhelming feeling I got was one of violence.

As I look back on that experience, I believe these feelings were spirits of influence, the powers that Paul has in mind here. By the way, many missionaries believe the controlling spirit over America is materialism.

There is a third order or rank or grouping of demonic spirits here in Ephesians 6: *rulers of the darkness of this world.* These are demons assigned to men and women in leadership to influence their decisions for the kingdom of darkness. I believe even pastors have a demon assigned to them.

The final group is *spiritual wickedness in high places.* These seem to be spirits associated with religion. Did you know that more people around the world are turning to New Age teaching than are turning to Christ? That's even true in the former Soviet Union and the countries of Eastern Europe which have so recently been freed from communism.

How do you account for this? There is no world headquarters for the New Age movement. They don't send out missionaries. I don't think you can explain this kind of thing in merely human terms.

Consider the unquestioning loyalty of the Branch Davidians outside Waco, Texas in early 1993. The authorities had to restrain David Koresh's people from running back into the building to be burned up. Consider also the willingness of most parents to give their children poisoned Kool-Aid at the command of Jim Jones in Guyana. Would any parent normally do that? The only explanation for such behavior—a kind of religious fanaticism and delusion that resulted in senseless death—is demonic influence.

The Evil Day

When you look at all of these forces arrayed against us, it's no wonder we need the whole armor of God! We need to apply the armor to withstand spiritual attacks during the "evil day" (v. 13). This is not a twenty-four-hour period. I like the definition given by Kenneth Wuest, the Greek professor for so many years at Moody Bible Institute. He says the evil day is a particular day, a day of violent temptations and attacks whenever they come to us. Remember we saw that in Luke 4, Satan left Jesus until an "opportune time," until another day when he could unleash his worst attacks.

So the "evil day" Paul has in mind here is the day when the great attack comes, when all hell breaks loose. When our friend Bill went back home after coming to freedom from his awful form of sexual bondage, I told him that an evil day would come for him.

Nothing particular happened for about three months. Then one day Bill called me and said he been asked to go to the local high school to take measurements for some architectural renovations the school wanted to make. For some reason, he told me, he had a bad feeling about the assignment, although there was nothing especially significant about it.

When Bill went to the school to do the measurements, the students were putting on a play in the school theater, which meant he was not able to measure that part of the school. He would have to go back a second time to measure the theater. He called me again and asked me to pray for him.

Bill arrived at the school theater and began his work. As he made his way along, he noticed some rooms off to the side of the theater, which also needed measuring. He turned the external light switch to one room, stepped inside, and quickly discovered a room filled with the very items he used when he practiced his sexual bondage. The items themselves were harmless, and I don't want to leave the wrong impression about the school. But seeing all the clothing and miscellaneous items before him, Bill was suddenly confronted with his "evil day."

He told me later that the temptation was so strong he could almost hear a voice saying, "Go ahead, just this one time. It won't hurt you just to touch them." But praise the Lord, Bill resisted the tempter in the name of Christ and walked out.

Everything was fine until the next Valentine's Day, which was near Bill's one-year anniversary of freedom. He came under sustained attacks at home, at work, at church, and everywhere else he went that day.

He called me and said, "Jim, it's bad. I don't know if I can make it." But the Lord gave him more grace, and Bill stood firm. After that day the intense attacks stopped. Bill's experience reinforces the nature of the evil day, which Bible scholar Clinton Arnold describes as specific times when the enemy's attack comes with extraordinary power and the temptation to yield is exceptionally strong.

That, my friend, is spiritual warfare! And since the "evil day" doesn't come just once (as much as we wish it would), we need to keep our armor in good repair.

The Christian's Armor

Now we are ready to consider the Christian's armor, one important piece at a time:

> Stand therefore, having your loins girt about with truth, and having on the breastplate of righteousness; and your feet shod with the preparation of the gospel of peace; above all, taking the shield of faith, wherewith ye shall be able to quench all the fiery darts of the wicked. And take the helmet of salvation, and the sword of the Spirit, which is the word of God. (Ephesians 6:14-17)

The Belt of Truth

The first piece of armor in the believer's arsenal is the belt of truth. The belt is what held the Roman soldier's armor together. When it comes to the truth, you have only two choices. Either you will believe what you perceive to be the truth, or you will embrace and believe God's truth.

Why do we need to put on the belt of truth? To answer that, all we need to do is ask, who is it we will meet today? Satan, the "father of lies," that great deceiver! The only way to stand against a liar or a deceiver is with the truth.

Remember, a liar will keep coming at you with his lies as long as they work. Why shouldn't he? Suppose you were to drive home from work one night and see a scraggly-looking man standing outside your front door. You park in your driveway, get out of your car, and walk up to your front door. This stranger puts out his hand and demands five dollars before he will allow you to enter your own home. If you give him the money, guess what? He'll be back again the next night. And if you give him five more dollars, he'll be right there waiting for you again the night after that.

In fact, this man will keep coming back as long as his lie works. But if you know the truth that this is your home and he has no right to be there, you can say to him, "Get out of here, or I'll call a higher authority."

That's the way Satan works—and he'll keep it up until we call his bluff. If we don't have the belt of truth firmly buckled around our waist, nothing else fits. But as God's people we are well-equipped in this area. We have truth incarnate in the person of the Lord Jesus (John 14:6), the Spirit of truth (John 14:17), the Word of truth (2 Corinthians 6:7), and the church, which is the "pillar and ground of the truth" (1 Timothy 3:15).

One other thing about the truth. If God's truth is this important, you can be sure Satan will make you too busy to read your Bible.

Breastplate of Righteousness

The second piece of spiritual armor is the breastplate of righteousness (v. 14). This protects us against the work of Satan as the "accuser." The righteousness referred to here could either be our righteousness or Christ's. I believe Paul is referring to Christ's righteousness, which He gives to us in exchange for our sin (2 Corinthians 5:21).

The reason for this is that when it comes to standing against the accuser, Christ is the only person who is totally blameless. Satan could point at no sin in Christ's life (John 14:30), whereas you and I have plenty of things in our lives Satan can accuse us of, even things we have been forgiven of by Christ.

That's why we need to stand with Christ's righteousness around us like a breastplate. When we stand in Christ, Satan has nothing to touch in us, nothing to accuse us of. The enemy and his underlings aren't afraid of us, but they're afraid of Christ.

The Sandals

In verse 15 Paul turns his attention to our feet, urging us to put on the third piece of spiritual armor, the sandals of the gospel of peace. This is not just going out to preach the gospel. That's not the context here. The subject on the floor is spiritual warfare, so I believe Paul has in mind our need to resist the attacks of the enemy and stand in Christ's peace.

"My peace I give unto you," Jesus said (John 14:27). Why do you need to put on the sandals of peace today? Because you are going to meet a "roaring lion" called Satan (1 Peter 5:8), who will try to make your feet slip by convincing you that God doesn't care about you. In fact, the enemy is "seeking whom he may devour" (v. 8). Literally, Satan wants "to gulp you down quickly."

Do you know how a lion uses his fearsome roar to frighten his prey? I'm told that the old male in a lion pride goes upwind of a herd of gazelles or whatever and lets out a roar. The terrified animals take off in the opposite direction, where the rest of the pride is waiting to gobble them up.

If we were to hear a lion roar, most of us would run. If he roared again, we would run again. Pretty soon we're being directed by fear. Jesus says, "Don't do that. Stand in the peace I give you."

Peter repeats that promise in the preceding verse. He assures us that we can cast all our cares upon God, "for he careth for you" (v. 7). This phrase can be translated, "You are a matter of concern to God."

I've seen the importance of the "sandals of peace" many times in my counseling ministry. People engaged in intense spiritual warfare, especially those who are being wiped out day after day, sometimes conclude, "God doesn't really care about me. If He did, He wouldn't let me languish in this terrible bondage." But Peter says emphatically, God cares! You and I are the objects of His deep concern. A Wycliffe Bible Translators' missionary once told me that when he translated 1 Peter 5:7 into a Mayan Indian dialect it came out, "What concerns you concerns Him." What a wonderful promise!

That promise is so important because, remember, we're talking about warfare. If you were in a battle in the ancient world, where the fighting was one-on-one, you had better be well-shod. There would be nothing worse than losing your footing with an enemy standing over you, sword in hand.

Even in modern warfare, how you walk is critical. Just ask any Vietnam War veteran how easy it was to step on a booby trap or land mine. If you had to walk through a field laced with hundreds of hidden mines waiting to blow your foot off, how would you walk? Carefully!

Would you want to know at a time like that that you were a matter of intense concern to God? I think you would. So would I. This is exactly the assurance that the sandals of God's peace provide us if we will put them on. Isn't it interesting that in a discussion of warfare, Paul brings up the subject of peace?

I believe these first three pieces of armor are positional truth. I have these things by virtue of being a Christian. I simply have to recall them, accept their truth, and respond accordingly. But the next four pieces are not positional. I have to take them up, put them on. There's a change of verb tense here. It's more active.

Shield of Faith

"Above all," Paul says, we are to take the shield of faith (v. 16). This phrase may suggest that the shield of faith is the most important piece of our spiritual armor. The shield covered the soldier, giving him overall protection against the enemy's darts and arrows. Faith is so important to us because it gives us:

F — Forgiveness of sin
A — Assurance of salvation
I — Identification in God's family
T — Triumph over Satan
H — Hope of deliverance

At its simplest, faith is believing what God has said. Why do we stand against the enemy? Because God tells us to. We stand in the strength of what He says, not what we think. My ideas are not what is important here.

As I said back in chapter 4 in relation to forgiveness, obedience precedes understanding. Faith demands a warrant, a grounds for belief. A warrant, as we noted, is a legal document that gives someone permission to do something. If someone wanted to search your home, you would probably demand that he show you his search warrant, a legal document giving him the right to do so. He receives such a warrant only when he can provide evidence that something probably will be found during the search.

In Hebrews 11 we see a whole array of men and women who are referred to in connection with their faith. Their actions were based on what God said (the warrant), and God held them up as men and women of faith.

There's a great picture of this truth in Mark 4, where Jesus and the disciples encountered a fierce storm. We read in verse 39 that Jesus "rebuked" the wind, which by the way is the same word for what He always did to the demons.

Then He turned to the disciples and asked, "Why are ye so fearful?

HIGHER GROUND:
Wearing Spiritual Armor

In his book *Winning the War Within*, Pastor Charles Stanley reveals that he begins each day by putting on the armor through prayer, one piece at a time.[1] Here are some ideas to help you make a similar prayer part of your daily spiritual routine.

1. Tell God that, by faith, you put on His belt of truth this day. Reject any thought or suggestion that does not line up with His truth, no matter what your feelings or your senses may be telling you. Thank God also that you have come to know the truth about Him (Ephesians 4:21) and about yourself.

2. Prayerfully put on the breastplate of righteousness. Ask God to help you keep your breastplate in place today to guard your heart and emotions, to keep you from being attracted to anything that is impure. Set your heart and mind on what is true and good and pure (Philippians 4:8).

3. Put on the sandals of the gospel of peace, so you can walk with a sure step and not be tripped up by the enemy. Pray that you will display God's peace wherever you go.

4. Take up up the shield of faith, so that you can stand against the enemy. Thank God that your faith is not groundless, but has a warrant, a grounds for action. Claim His promise to give you the strength you need to repel the incoming "flaming missiles" of the enemy.

5. Place upon your head the helmet of salvation, which is the hope of God's deliverance. Thank the Lord that He has provided you with this piece of protection against the enemy's lie that your situation is hopeless, that there is no way out.

6. Strap on your sword of the Spirit, God's Word. Thank God for the precious gift of His Word and rejoice that His Spirit can give you a Word for your immediate need. Determine that you will spend time in the Word today to increase your arsenal of truth.

7. Pray with supplication. Pray for your prayer targets, the people God has put on your heart.

how is it that ye have no faith?" (v. 40). This must have been a terrible storm, because these guys were veteran sailors. But the key to Jesus' question is found back in verse 35. He had said they were going to the other side of the Sea of Galilee, not going out to the middle and drown.

So the real problem was that the disciples didn't believe Jesus. They doubted His word, and He had to rebuke them for it. The shield of faith quenches those darts of doubt Satan will throw at us. In the ancient world, a shield was an absolute necessity. Roman soldiers even interlocked their shields for more protection.

Helmet of Salvation

Next is the helmet of salvation (v. 17). The word *salvation* here can also be translated "deliverance," and I believe that's exactly the idea Paul has in mind here. If your child runs into the street and I run after him, pull him out of the path of a car, and bring him back to you, what are you most likely to say? "Thanks for saving him."

What I did has nothing to do with eternity. Passages like 1 Thessalonians 5:8 talk about the "helmet, the hope of salvation." Here in Ephesians 6, Paul is not worried about the enemy stealing away our salvation, nor is he saying that we can only hope we are saved. Satan can't steal our salvation because our hope in Christ is certain, not a mere wish.

The helmet of salvation, in other words, is the hope of deliverance. Why do we need this? Because as we've seen throughout the book, Satan wants us to believe our situation is hopeless.

Remember, if you believe your situation is hopeless, if you become convinced that you are trapped in your bondage and there's nothing you can do, you only have two choices. You can either abandon yourself to the sin, or get ready to check out of this life! When I begin to believe the enemy's lie, God says I need to put on the helmet.

Sword of the Spirit

The next piece of spiritual armor is the sword of the Spirit. This item has often been misunderstood and misinterpreted. Paul is referring to the *memorized* Word of God, not the Bible. The Holy Spirit can't bring to your mind what isn't there.

This is the *rhema* of God, not the *logos*. A *rhema* is the word for an immediate need (see page 173). This means knowing and quoting Scriptures under the influence of the Holy Spirit, not merely saying words as part of a simple formula. Words are not magic. Notice that it is the sword of the *Spirit.* It's the sword *He* uses, not us. The Holy Spirit is the one who empowers the Word when we quote Scripture to the enemy.

Therefore, the sword of the Spirit won't be of any use to us in spiritual warfare if we're grieving or quenching the Holy Spirit. Some people get very mystical here. I know of one man who slept with the Bible on his chest to protect him. How silly. You might as well open your Bible to John 3:16 and slide it under your bed at night. That's occultic, not scriptural. I should also mention that using the rhema of the Spirit does not demand that we quote every verse of Scripture word-perfect. The power is in the truth of the Scriptures. When we come against the enemy with the truth of God, he has to flee.

Praying with Supplication

Our final piece of spiritual armor is found in Ephesians 6:18: "praying always with all prayer and supplication in the Spirit." A good way I have found to implement the armor of praying *with supplication* is to develop what I call prayer targets.

The idea behind prayer targets is that they give you another line of defense against the enemy's attacks. We have already said that whatever your area or areas of weakness in temptation, you want to develop an arsenal of verses to deal with them. I suggest that you choose verses to fortify yourself against all three of the major categories of temptation the apostle John lists in 1 John 2:16: "the lust of the flesh, and the lust of the eyes, and the pride of life."

Once you have your sword of the Spirit, God's Word, well in hand, then select a prayer target for each of your areas of weakness. Let me show you how this works.

A prayer target is a person you know: either a believer, an unbeliever, or a backslider. Whenever the enemy attacks you with a destructive temptation, counterattack by praying for your targeted person. Pray that this person will be turned around and do great damage to Satan and his kingdom.

For example, suppose I have a real weakness in the area of anger. And I have a friend who really needs Christ. Each time I am tempted to explode in anger and I resist, the Holy Spirit brings this friend to mind as part of my resistance to the tempter and his temptation to anger. I begin praying that God will bring this person to Himself, and that this friend will then do great damage to Satan and his kingdom. It's hard to stay angry when you're praying for someone else.

Prayer targets are a very simple concept, but I can tell you they will revolutionize your prayer life, to say nothing of helping make you stronger in the battle. We need to do more than just try and duck Satan's onslaughts. Wielding the sword of the Spirit and praying for my prayer targets puts me on the offensive, the counterattack, when Satan strikes. That's where I want to be, not ducking or backpedaling.

— 15 —
THE BATTLE
IS IN YOUR HEAD

Spiritual warfare is a battle for the mind. This is the final truth we want to consider about spiritual warfare, and it may be the most important.

The fact that the warfare is a battle for the mind should not surprise you, based on all that's been said so far about the way the enemy attacks us and gains ground in our lives. Protecting our minds from his onslaughts is vital because sin begins as a thought. A suggestion, an idea, a tempting possibility—whatever it takes, Satan wants to bring some plan to your mind to get you and me to act upon.

Fortifying our minds for effective spiritual warfare is the final step in the process we've been describing whereby we take back any ground yielded to Satan and begin clearing that ground of the strongholds he has built.

Once we have moved from spiritual defeat to spiritual victory, the goal is to live day by day in that victory. We can only do that as we replace Satan's strongholds of lies with towers of truth to which we can flee when the enemy attacks.

You might say, then, that getting control of our minds and turning them into effective spiritual weapons in the power of the Holy Spirit is the stage in spiritual warfare where we go on the offensive. Once I have taken back ground surrendered to the enemy and have destroyed his strongholds, I want to keep him from stealing back any of that ground the next time he comes around. That's why our minds are so crucial.

The Battle for the Mind

To help you in this important area, I want to talk first about the mind under attack, the battle we're facing for our minds. Some of this will, of necessity, be review, because we've already looked at some of the ways Satan comes against our minds. But these truths are so crucial to understand that I don't think it will hurt if we repeat a point or two made earlier. Then we will consider how we can renew our minds as Christians, as Paul tells us to in Romans 12:1–2. I want to give you a biblical "battle plan" that includes what it means to renew your mind, how you can take control of your thoughts, and how to set your mind on those thoughts that please God and are according to His Word.

So let's begin as we seek to obey Peter's command to "gird up the loins of your mind" (1 Peter 1:13), a figure of speech that pictures a person in the ancient world tucking the ends of his flowing garment into his waistband so he will be free for action. An equivalent exhortation in our day would be, "Roll up your sleeves and get to work!"

That's a great picture of what God wants us to do with our minds. There is nothing passive about spiritual warfare, especially when it comes to guarding and fortifying the mind. I like the way one Bible scholar defines the mind in 1 Peter 1:13: It is "the center of understanding that produces thoughts and resolves, the power of rational judgment which can be swayed by outside factors such as the appeal of evil desires (v. 14)."[1]

There's a lot of truth in that sentence. What he is saying is right in line with what we said earlier about our thoughts. Remember, thoughts can come from one of three sources: ourselves, God, or Satan. Woe be to the person who cannot tell the difference. Satan's great scheme is to plant his intruding thoughts in our minds, make us think they are our thoughts, and then accuse us for having them.

This is why 2 Corinthians 10:3–5 is such a vital passage of Scripture to understand. Have you ever put these verses side-by-side with Romans 12:2? These two texts are wholly consistent. What they tell us is that there is a false belief system out there that seeks to capture us and squeeze us into its mold, a system shaped by all the influences around and within us that the Bible calls the "world" and the "flesh."

I said in an earlier chapter that each of us has within him a belief system that is the product of these influences—family, education, media, peers, music, etc. I am not suggesting by any means that everything we receive through these sources is false. Not at all. However, our false perceptions based on these influences must be replaced by a belief system based on truth if our behavior is to be acceptable to God.

Why? Because we draw on our belief system to formulate our decisions and actions. What kind of decisions and actions will come from a badly flawed belief system? Badly flawed decisions and actions!

Our friend Bill is a classic example. As long as he believed that he was hopelessly trapped in his sexual problem and was slowly destroying his family too, the only rational decision seemed to be to do away with himself. God had to change Bill's belief system, his mind, before Bill could come to freedom.

According to Proverbs 23:7, "As [a person] thinketh in his heart, so is he." In essence, it is impossible for a person to live inconsistently with his belief system. A person may not always live what he professes, but he will always act in accord with what he believes.

So our challenge is to refocus and reprogram our minds, to replace wrong thoughts with right and God-honoring thoughts. We'll conclude the chapter, and the book in fact, by looking at Paul's "recommended thinking" list in Philippians 4:8. But we're not ready for that yet.

Two Actions to Take

Let's return to 2 Corinthians 10:3–5, which contains truths that are essential to winning the battle for the mind. Notice first the strong context of warfare. These verses alert us that we are in a very real battle, and that the battleground is the mind of the Christian.

I see two important actions here that are absolutely vital to carry out if we are to win the battle for our minds. The first is that we must yield our minds to the control of the Holy Spirit. The importance of being Spirit-filled is spelled out elsewhere in Scripture (Ephesians 5:18). We belong to the Lord body, soul, and spirit, and it is the Holy Spirit who indwells us to empower us for obedience. So it follows that our minds must be placed under His control. What's the alternative to a Spirit-controlled mind? A "carnal" or fleshly mind, and Paul tells us in verse 4 that weapons of the flesh are utterly useless in spiritual warfare.

The second action we must take is to accept God's Word as our final authority. Why is this important when it comes to tearing down Satan's strongholds in our minds? Because these strongholds are reinforced by feelings. In my own life, I didn't just believe I was inferior. I felt strongly inferior for many years, and this feeling had a devastating effect on my ministry and my personal walk with Christ.

Here's where a believer's commitment to the authority of the Word makes the difference. I had a decision to make. Was I going to hold on to my wrong belief and wrong feelings about myself, or was I going to believe God's objective, written truth to me that I was a person of worth and value in His sight? You have faced those same kinds of decisions, I'm sure. In my case, I had to make a new choice if anything was going to happen in my life. I had to decide to believe God minus the feelings, or hang on to my wrong beliefs reinforced by wrong feelings.

It comes down to this: Is God worthy of our trust, and is His Word the final authority in our lives? God, by His grace, enabled me to trust Him and believe His Word. As I did that, the stronghold of inferiority was pulled down in my life.

Two Battles to Fight

In addition to two actions, I see two battles in 2 Corinthians 10:3–5. The first is the one I have just described, the "pulling down of strong holds" (v. 4).

The second battle here is called "bringing into captivity every thought to the obedience of Christ" (v. 5). If anyone thinks spiritual warfare is a passive affair where we just empty our minds and let God fill them, this verse is a corrective to that. This is a verse of action. The idea behind the word *captivity* is that we are to take our thoughts "at spear point."

I think what M. R. Vincent has to say about verse 5 in his *Word Studies in the New Testament* is very helpful. He calls the strongholds "high military works thrown up, or lofty, natural fortresses with their battlements of rock." Bringing our thoughts into captivity, he says, continues the military metaphor. "The obedience [of Christ] is the new stronghold into which the captives are led."[2]

Isn't that a great picture? The new strongholds Vincent is talking about are the same thing we have been calling towers of truth. The insight he shares is so valuable because the idea is not just to liberate our thoughts from Satan's control so they can float freely. As sinful people, our thoughts still need to be brought into captivity and obedience. The goal is to submit our minds to the right commander.

Discerning the Source of Our Thoughts

But this also raises a question. If we are to take our thoughts captive, how do we know when we've captured an intruding thought from the enemy and either need to turn it around or get rid of it? What do wrong thoughts look like? I can't do a lot to take my thoughts captive for Christ if I can't distinguish among my thoughts.

Identifying Wrong Thoughts

One reason this is so important is that we as believers can fall victim to what appear to be good thoughts. They may even be religious thoughts, telling us to do seemingly good things. The difference is that when these thoughts are from the enemy, they come with a strong coercive force that is much different than the gentle constraining of the Holy Spirit's direction. I think you'll see that difference in the testimony below.

But because these thoughts come in a religious guise, it never occurs to most of us to question their origin. As I often remind my counselees, however, the enemy doesn't care what tool he uses to ensnare us, as long as he gets us bound up and renders us useless.

A Case Study

This idea may be a little hard to get hold of, so let me tell Alan's story. A pastor of a small church in Texas, Alan is an earnest believer, who also has a full-time secular job to provide for his wife and their two small girls.

Like many Christians who are driven to work very hard, Alan worked diligently and sincerely for the Lord, but felt no joy or other fruit of the Spirit because his efforts were not Spirit-directed. Alan's childhood was typical of many small-town boys. He was raised in a country church, and made a profession of faith at the age of eight. Notably, before Alan was born, his mother went through a period of severe legalism in her faith. She got rid of everything that might be worldly, removing all the pictures from the walls in their house. Amazingly, wanting to do what was "right," at one point she even consulted a palm reader.

According to Alan, his mom left this particular movement soon after he was born, but he was plagued with very strong and compulsive thoughts from a very early age. He describes it as being "legalistically driven." At the age of six or seven, he felt a very strong sense of the need to get involved in church.

When Alan came under conviction and was led to give his heart to Christ, he says he remembers not wanting to go forward to make a public profession. He told the Lord, "I'll work for You, but I don't want to go forward." Alan was baptized that same year, and says that even then he was committed to whatever God wanted to him to do. This high level of commitment stayed with him, but he became extremely legalistic about everything. In his written testimony, he explained how this legalism manifested itself:

> If I read Scripture, I had to read every word and so many verses every day. I wasn't reading for the joy of reading God's Word. I became very critical of others, and felt like I had to tell everyone else what to do. Once, I saw another boy at church taking communion in what I felt was not the proper attitude of reverence, and I got so mad I actually shook my fist at him.
>
> My compulsiveness also spilled over into other areas that had nothing to do with religion. I had to touch things with both hands, for example. I either had to step over a crack in the sidewalk or step on it with both feet.

Remember, this is a young boy we're talking about. Can you see how the enemy was setting Alan up for problems later in life? Alan was

HIGHER GROUND:
Renewing Your Mind

A mind in tune with God is more able to stand against Satan's attack. Mind renewal (Romans 12:2) is crucial, and this six-part list shows how to open your mind to God's control. (See also pages 196–98 for an action plan you can follow to daily renew your mind and stay on top of the spiritual battle.

1. Acknowledge the lies, negative thoughts, accusations, and doubts as no longer being true of you as a new creation in Christ (2 Corinthians 5:17).

2. Ask God's forgiveness for any lingering resentment, anger, hatred, and bitterness you may hold against people who have hurt or sinned against you. Freely forgive them that God may freely forgive you (Mark 11:25).

3. Turn back the enemy's lies as attempts to thwart your growth and freedom in Christ. Put off your old self (Ephesians 4:22).

4. Immerse your mind and heart in God's truth. Spend time in portions of Scripture that speak to your soul; claim His promises by faith.

5. Ask the Holy Spirit to strengthen you. Thank God for what He is doing in your life (Ephesians 5:20). Praise and bless the Lord (Psalms 16:7; 34:1).

6. Rest in the assurance that, as you are faithful, God will do the work of renewing your mind.

not hearing any voices or anything that could be classified as unusual. These were just very strong, compelling thoughts that he never questioned. He assumed they were a normal part of growing up.

One clue that something was wrong was that Alan never had any sense of joy in his early Christian life. In fact, he says he was miserably unhappy during those years, even though he was doing everything he thought God wanted him to do.

In his early teens Alan struggled with the assurance of his salvation at the same time as he was struggling to serve God with zeal. The more doubt he felt, the more zealous he became to serve. "The enemy wanted to rob me of any semblance of peace and joy and make me a slave to religion, a religious zealot who served out of a sense of fear and guilt instead of love," Alan says in looking back on those years.

By the way, what Alan describes is also characteristic of many members of religious cults who get caught up in the terrible legalism of these false systems. Here the enemy uses his intruding thoughts to do great damage, because most people assume that if they are being driven to do religious things, that's good.

Alan, of course, was not a cultist. He was a sincere and confused teenager who knew the Lord but who was caught in the merry-go-round of feeling like he just had to do certain things—thoughts that he now recognizes as coming from the enemy. Given his compulsion to set other people straight, it's not surprising that in high school, Alan was known as "preacher" and became something of a loner. He was very argumentative and judgmental, trying hard to be a witness as best he knew but coming at things the wrong way.

Alan was also hard on his sister, who was four years younger than he. By this time his mother was hardly going to church at all, and his father kept to himself out in the garage when he wasn't working. The whole family was affected by this legalistic spirit, even long after Alan's mother had left her legalistic practices.

Looking back on his college years, Alan can see how the enemy had been setting him up for a fall. Up to this point, Alan had been compulsively religious and had lived a very strict life. But in college, he encountered pornography and fell into the trap of sexual sin. Instead of being horrified by it and driven the other way, Alan tried to justify his moral compromises. He told himself he had lived a good life and deserved a little pleasure. He would make vows to God and bargain with Him, but all the time he was yielding more and more ground to the enemy.

What's really interesting is that as Alan gave in morally, his religious doubts went away—which, as he says, tells you where those doubts were coming from. The enemy had used intruding thoughts to keep Alan in religious bondage, a zealot who worked for God out of a sense of duty. And to keep Alan really tied up, Satan flooded his mind with doubts that robbed him of any sense of peace or joy.

As Alan was completing college, new direction came into his life. At age twenty-one, he dated a special woman. They soon married and eventually had a child. During this time Alan came to grips with his sin, but he did not understand how to deal with the enemy's involvement in his life. He says he believed that God was going to take his life for his sin. He began having serious physical problems: chest pains, difficulty breathing, anxiety attacks.

Despite all of this, Alan still had a heart to serve Christ. He became involved in youth work and eventually was asked to serve a small church as the interim pastor. But soon he felt himself burdened by guilt over his life.

"Satan took the role of the accuser in my life," Alan says. "He loaded me with guilt and made me feel unworthy to be a pastor. It was really wearing me out." He called a Christian organization and was referred to me, and Alan and I had a lengthy conversation before he agreed to see me. "I want to be healed of these physical problems," he told me, "but I also want be free of the unhappiness that seems to have been part of my Christian life from the beginning."

We spent a week together at a later point. I emphasized our acceptance in Christ and our honored position in Him. We discussed where his spiritual battle lay, and I led Alan through the steps to freedom. The two keys to freedom were Alan being able to recognize the source of his spiritual battles and to accept his physical limitation as part of God's wise plan.

"Seeing where my spiritual warfare was gave me a strong foundation and the strength to go on. As I took back the ground, the intruding thoughts went away," Alan later wrote.

"Of course, I wanted my physical problems to go away too, but a real key for me was seeing them in the light of following the Lord. I came to the point that I was willing to accept my physical limitations because, like Paul, I could see that God would produce something good from it (2 Corinthians 12)."

Alan began to see what was important: that God loved him and wanted His best for him, that he was in Christ, and that the enemy was under his feet. These truths revolutionized Alan's life and preaching, and even though he still suffers physically his ministry is fruitful and full of joy.

Recognizing Satan's Attacks

What Alan experienced is just one of the ways Satan can attack our minds. The Scripture gives us other examples of how Satan can come against the mind, not only of believers but of unbelievers as well. Satan can darken or blind the mind (Ephesians 4:17–18; 2 Corinthians 4:3–4), corrupt the mind ((2 Corinthians 11:3), deceive with his wiles (Ephesians 6:11), prevent understanding of the Word (Mark 4:15), and come as an angel of light to spread darkness (2 Corinthians 11:14). Satan even engages in a seduction, as he uses "seducing spirits" to lead the mind away from the truth to a lie (1 Timothy 4:1).

What a contrast to the way the Scripture describes a mind in tune with God and under the control of the Holy Spirit, one that is ready and eager to receive the truth of God's Word (Acts 17:11). This kind of mind produces humility (Acts 20:19; Colossians 3:12); it is a spiritual mind (Romans 8:6), a willing mind (2 Corinthians 8:12), a sound mind (2 Timothy 4:1), and a pure mind (2 Peter 3:1).

In short, a mind in tune with God and under the control of the Holy Spirit is a renewed mind. Let's find out how we can renew our minds as God intends and win this all-important battle, the great ongoing battle in spiritual warfare.

Renewing Our Minds

The primary exhortation to us to renew our minds is found in Romans 12:2. But the apostle Paul's plea for mind renewal actually begins in verse 1, with a call to present our bodies to God as a living sacrifice. The place to start in renewing our minds is to make a complete surrender of ourselves to the Lord—body, soul, and spirit, which includes our minds.

I believe this has to be a daily attitude of surrender. As a number of people have observed, the trouble with a living sacrifice is that it keeps crawling off the altar. Our minds are certainly alive and active, taking in and processing thoughts every day. That's why for the Christian, mind renewal is one of the everyday disciplines of spiritual warfare. The good news is that we can train our minds the way we train our bodies. It's a positive process, not simply a matter of emptying our heads of bad thoughts. We are never told in Scripture to empty our minds. In fact, Jesus warned about the danger of a mind that is empty and swept in relation to demonic activity (see Matthew 12:45).

Some Important Reminders

We've already identified the three sources of our thoughts: ourselves, the Lord, and the enemy. Let me remind you here that you do not need to be dominated by your old way of thinking. Your thoughts are not authoritative. Having a thought says nothing about who or what you are. To accept your thoughts as authoritative is to set yourself up for real problems.

Also, the mere presence of a thought in your mind does not mean you have to obey it. Neither does the presence of a thought mean that it will happen. We do not create reality by our thought life. I am repeating these things here because so many people believe that if they think something, they are bound to carry it out, or that thinking the thought somehow gives them freedom to commit the deed.

A final reminder I want to leave with you before we get into the discipline of renewing the mind is this: simply having a wrong thought does not make you sinful or guilty. If it did, Jesus would be sinful, as He received (but did not act upon) wrong thoughts, which were suggested to Him by Satan in the temptation in the wilderness.

It's true that the devil will not yield his control over a person's thought life without a fight, so we should be prepared for spiritual warfare when we declare war on our old way of thinking. But the battle has already been won for us. We have been set free. God has given us a "sound mind" (2 Timothy 1:7).

A Daily Discipline for Mind Renewal

As you can tell by now, I like to talk about specific, achievable steps people can take to get where God wants them to be. This is true when it comes to obeying Romans 12:1–2, so let me suggest some steps that have helped thousands of men and women to take charge of their thinking and bring their minds under the control of the Holy Spirit.

1. Test your thoughts. "Try the spirits whether they are of God" (1 John 4:1). Get used to the process of examining your thoughts to determine their origin. The source of some thoughts will be readily obvious if they are vile and wicked. But as we saw in Alan's case, the origin of other thoughts is not so obvious.

We have the ministry of the Spirit to help us in this process, but too many believers have never engaged their minds to cooperate with the Spirit. It was Plato who said the unexamined life is not worth living. We could paraphrase this and say the unexamined thought is not worth thinking. (Of course, when examining our thoughts, we do not try to chase down the source of every thought that passes through our minds. That would be impossible anyway. Instead, we're dealing with those thoughts that crowd their way into our conscious thinking and have some sort of effect on our actions.)

Thankfully, God has not left us on our own to try and figure things out. His Word gives us the standard by which to test every thought. We don't need to fall into the trap of believing that God is just sort of open-minded about things, that if something is beautiful and true to me, this is all that matters. God's truth doesn't work that way. What is the first piece of spiritual armor the Christian is to put on? The belt of truth (Ephesians 6:14).

2. Refuse wrong thoughts. The fact that we have the power in Christ to say no to wrong thoughts is an eye-opening revelation to many whom I counsel. By the time they come to my office, many of these people are so used to being in bondage to wrong thinking that it never occurs to them they have the power to refuse to obey their wrong thoughts.

There is an important distinction we need to keep in mind here: the difference between thoughts and thinking. The enemy can plant wrong thoughts in our minds, but he cannot force us to think about them, to mull them over and let them germinate into full-fledged sin.

I believe this distinction is what James 1:14–15 is talking about. Lust has to "conceive" to produce sin. That is, we have to feed and nourish a lustful thought before it can produce anything. I encourage my counselees, and I encourage you, to use this simple affirmation when a wrong thought comes: "I give no consent to that."

3. Resist the devil. We've dealt with this in enough detail that I don't need to add much more here. But resistance needs to be included in our daily mind renewal process because Satan does not always flee at our first effort to say no to him. We have the authority and power of Christ, though, to command the enemy to leave.

4. Share every thought with the Lord immediately. This is very important when it comes to the kinds of thoughts Satan most often uses to trip us up: the memories of past sins and failures. If such sin is under the blood of Christ and you have dealt with its consequences, the enemy has no authority to afflict you with it. You can give that accusing thought to Christ and thank Him that He died to cleanse you.

5. Memorize God's Word. We could do an entire chapter on the incredible value and importance of Scripture memory. We keep coming back to the importance of replacing wrong thoughts with right ones— and the only infallible source of right thoughts is God's Word. Scripture memory is one of those daily disciplines that has a wonderful cumulative effect on your mind and heart. As you soak your mind in Scripture, you begin to think God's thoughts. And you give the Holy Spirit a tremendous arsenal of truth to draw upon and bring to your mind when you are in a time of need.

6. Set your mind on things above. A wonderful New Testament verse acts as a biblical "catalog" of what God wants us to think about. Here is the catalog description:

> Brethren, whatsoever things are true, whatsoever things are honest, whatsoever things are just, whatsoever things are pure, whatsoever

things are lovely, whatsoever things are of good report; if there be any virtue, and if there be any praise, think on these things. (Philippians 4:8)

I can't think of a better way to close our study than to consider each of these terms Paul uses and see how God wants us to use our minds.

"Whatsoever things are true." The idea of truth is that which conforms to reality from God's perspective, that which is genuine and accurate. The opposite of truth, by the way, is not falsehood. It is fantasy —that which is unreal, which does not conform to biblical reality.

"Whatsoever things are honest." This has to do with what is honorable, God-honoring, worthy of our reverence and esteem. It suggests that we should reject thoughts which are ignoble, mean, or unworthy of someone who is seeking to imitate the Lord Jesus Christ.

"Whatsoever things are just." In the Bible, the only true standard of what is just or right is God's righteousness. So to think what is right and do what is right, we must meditate on God's law, His Word (see Psalm 1:2).

"Whatsoever things are pure." This means uncontaminated, chaste, innocent, clean, free from all moral impurity. Obeying this standard alone would eliminate about half of the problems with our thought lives.

"Whatsoever things are lovely." This word suggests thoughts that are pleasing, agreeable, moving us and others toward love rather than toward that which is unlovely and unloving. Lovely (loving) thoughts lead to the kinds of actions that cause you to have an excellent reputation with others.

"Whatsoever things are of good report." The beautiful term *good report* means "well spoken of." It suggests a commitment to speak only that which is favorable about others. This does not deny the need to speak the truth in love when needed. Instead, what Paul has in mind here is the opposite of slander and gossip.

What a tremendous list! And what a call for us as God's people to conform our thinking to this pattern. The "virtue" and "praise" attached to thinking this way makes these the highest, most excellent thoughts we can have because they glorify God.

My closing challenge to you as a fellow believer is to make the renewal of your mind a daily discipline as you "war a good warfare." God will honor you for it, and you'll find spiritual power, authority, fruitfulness, and peace you never imagined were available to you.

Remember, a walk of spiritual victory is not a matter of one step at a time, but rather one choice at a time. God has given you all the resources you need to make that right choice!

NOTES

Introduction

1. Warren Wiersbe, *The Strategy of Satan* (Wheaton, Ill.: Tyndale, 1985), 105.

Chapter 2: Giving and Gaining Spiritual Ground

1. Neil Anderson, *Released from Bondage* (San Bernardino, Calif.: Here's Life, 1991), 15.

2. Timothy Warner, *Spiritual Warfare* (Wheaton, Ill.: Crossway, 1991), 79.

3. Ibid., 80.

4. Anderson, *Released from Bondage*, 16.

5. Warner, *Spiritual Warfare*, 79.

6. Scott Moreau, *The World of Spirits* (Nairobi, Kenya: Evangel Publishers, 1990), 90.

7. Frank Gaebelein, ed. *The Expositor's Bible Commentary*, vol. 11 (Grand Rapids, Mich.: Zondervan, 1978), 64.

8. Clinton Arnold, *The Powers of Darkness* (Downers Grove, Ill.: InterVarsity, 1992),128.

9. Ed Silvoso, "How to Reach Our Cities for Christ" videocassette (Oak Brook, Ill.: Institute in Basic Life Principles, 1992).

Chapter 6: What's So Terrible About Pride?

1. If you are not sure you are a Christian, I invite you to write to the Moody Press address at the end of this book for free literature on how to become a follower of Christ.

Chapter 8: Families Under Attack

1. Interestingly, this girl's mother has become a believer and her testimony is available on video. Contact the International Center for Biblical Counseling, 1551 Indian Hills Drive, Suite 200, Sioux City, IA, 51104, and we'll send information on obtaining a copy of this videotape. Or you may order it directly from Arrows Ministry, P. O. Box 992, Mission, SD 57555.

2. This missionary has made a video, "The Snake Story," in which he tells of his experiences on the field. Contact the International Center for Biblical Counseling at the above address for information on how to obtain this video, or you may order it directly from the Institute in Basic Life Principles, Box 1, Oak Brook, IL 60522.

Chapter 10: A Wife and Mother's Lasting Beauty

1. Gary Smalley, *If Only He Knew* (Grand Rapids, Mich.: Zondervan, 1988), 15.

2. H. Norman Wright, *Marriage & Family Enrichment Resource Manual* (Denver: Christian Marriage Enrichment, 1979), 58.

3. Ibid.

4. Smalley, *If Only He Knew,* 13–14.

Chapter 11: Children Can Resist Too

1. Here is a suggested prayer you can use for God's protection: "Heavenly Father, I ask You in the name and through the blood of the Lord Jesus Christ to bind and rebuke Satan, and to put a hedge of protection around me and each member of my family. I pray this in the confidence of Your Word, which says in Philippians 1:6, 'Being confident of this very thing, that he which hath begun a good work in you [us] will perform it until the day of Jesus Christ.' In the name of Jesus our Shepherd, amen."

2. Suspicious items would include reading materials or objects from false religions, occult objects, any sexually-oriented material, wrong music or videos, video games that involve evil, and New Age items. Destroying such materials is not an over-response; in fact it is what devout Christians did in Ephesus (Acts 19:19)

Chapter 14: What to Wear to the Battle

1. I love how Dr. Stanley closes his spiritual armor prayer each day, and I commend it to you: "Lord, I go now rejoicing that You have chosen me to represent You to this lost and dying world. May others see Jesus in me, and may Satan and his hosts shudder as Your power is made manifest in me. In Jesus' name I pray—AMEN" (page 125). I recommend Stanley's book, which is published by Thomas Nelson.

Chapter 15: The Battle Is in Your Head

1. Howard Marshall, *1 Peter, The IVP New Testament Commentary Series,* Grant R. Osborne, ed. (Downers Grove, Ill.: InterVarsity, 1991), 50–51.

2. M. R. Vincent, *Word Studies in the Greek New Testament* (Wilmington, Del.: Associated Publishers and Authors, 1972), 833–34.

SELECT
BIBLIOGRAPHY

Anderson, Neil T. *Living Free in Christ.* Ventura, Calif.: Regal, 1993.

Arnold, Clinton. *The Powers of Darkness.* Downers Grove, Ill.: InterVarsity, 1992.

Beeson, Ray. *The Real Battle.* Wheaton, Ill.: Tyndale, 1988.

Bubeck, Mark. *The Adversary.* Chicago: Moody, 1975.

_____. *Overcoming the Adversary.* Chicago: Moody, 1975.

_____. *The Satanic Revival.* San Bernardino, Calif.: Here's Life, 1991.

Bunyan, John. *The Pilgrim's Progress.* Chicago: Moody, 1984.

Carroll, Joseph S. *How to Worship Jesus Christ.* Chicago: Moody, 1991.

Crossman, Eileen. *Mountain Rain.* Littleton, Colo.: OMF Books, 1982.

Dickason, C. Fred. *Angels, Elect and Evil.* Chicago: Moody, 1975.

Gothard, Bill. *Life Purpose Journals* (vols. 1 & 3). Oak Brook, Ill.: Institute in Basic Life Principles, 1991.

Gurnall, William. *The Christian in Complete Armour.* Edited and Introduced by James S. Bell, Jr. Chicago: Moody, 1994.

Mathews, Arthur R. *Born for Battle.* Littleton, Colo.: OMF Books, 1985.

Murphy, Ed. *Handbook for Spiritual Warfare.* Nashville: Thomas Nelson, 1992.

Pentecost, J. Dwight. *Your Adversary, the Devil.* Grand Rapids, Mich.: Zondervan, 1969.

Peterson, Robert. *Roaring Lion.* Littleton, Colo.: OMF Books, 1969.

Stanley, Charles. *Winning the War Within.* Nashville: Oliver-Nelson, 1988.

Unger, Merrill F. *What Demons Can Do to Saints.* Chicago: Moody, 1991.

Warner, Timothy. *Spiritual Warfare.* Wheaton, Ill.: Crossway, 1991.

Watt, Gordon. *Effectual Fervent Prayer.* Greenville, S.C.: Great Commission Publishers, 1981.

Webster, Richard. *Tearing Down Strongholds.* Taipei, Taiwan: Campus Evangelical Fellowship, 1990.

—————. *Worship & Warfare.* Taipei, Taiwan: Campus Evangelical Fellowship, 1990.

White, Tom. *Breaking Strongholds.* Ann Arbor, Mich.: Servant, 1993.

Wiersbe, Warren W. *The Strategy of Satan.* Wheaton, Ill.: Tyndale, 1985.

—————. *What to Wear to the War.* Lincoln, Neb.: Back to the Bible, 1986.